THE
SOVIET UNION
AND INDIA

THE
SOVIET UNION
AND INDIA

Peter J.S. Duncan

PUBLISHED IN NORTH AMERICA FOR
THE ROYAL INSTITUTE OF INTERNATIONAL AFFAIRS

COUNCIL ON FOREIGN RELATIONS PRESS
NEW YORK

Chatham House Papers

General Series Editor: William Wallace
Soviet Foreign Policy Programme Director: Alex Pravda

The Royal Institute of International Affairs, at Chatham House in London, has provided an impartial forum for discussion and debate on current international issues for 70 years. Its resident research fellows, specialized information resources, and range of publications, conferences, and meetings span the fields of international politics, economics, and security. The Institute is independent of government.

Chatham House Papers are short monographs on current policy problems which have been commissioned by the RIIA. In preparing the papers, authors are advised by a study group of experts convened by the RIIA, and publication of a paper indicates that the Institute regards it as an authoritative contribution to the public debate. The Institute does not, however, hold opinions of its own; the views expressed in this publication are the responsibility of the author.

Library of Congress Cataloguing-in-Publication Data

Duncan, Peter J.S.. 1953–
    The Soviet Union and India/by Peter J.S. Duncan.
    p.   cm.—(Chatham House papers)
British ed. published in 1989 by the Institute and Routledge.
Bibliography: p.
ISBN 0-87609-062-5 : $14.95
1. Soviet Union —Relations—India.   2. India—Relations—Soviet Union.   3. Soviet Union—Foreign relations—1985–
I. Title.   II. Series: Chatham House papers (Unnumbered)
[DK68.7.I4D85   1989b]
327.47054—dc20   89-32088
                                                          CIP

89 90 91 92 93 94 95 PB 10 9 8 7 6 5 4 3 2 1

CONTENTS

ACKNOWLEDGMENTS

A large number of people helped me in this study – too many for me to be able to name them all. I am grateful for the aid of the diplomats, political leaders and government officials from several countries who provided me with background information but must remain anonymous.

The following research organizations generously extended help and hospitality to me: the Institute of World Economics and International Relations and the Institute of Oriental Studies in Moscow, the Indian Council of World Affairs, the Institute for Defence Studies and Analyses (New Delhi), the Indian Council for Social Science Research and the Pakistan Institute of International Affairs. The Centre of Soviet Studies at the University of Bombay organized a special seminar for me. I thank the directors and staff of all these bodies.

Among the individuals from other organizations who shared their knowledge with me were Inder Gujral, Bhabhani Sen Gupta, Ashen Choudhry, Govind Talwalkar, A.S. Abraham, Achin Vanaik, Ashok Mitra, D.R. Pendse, J.K. Mukhobadhyay, Zafar Imam, B. Vivekanandan, Bharat Wariavwalla, P.C. Joshi, P.M. Kamath, Paran Balakrishnan, K.V. Venkatasubramanyam and Mark Tully. In London I had the benefit of advice from a Chatham House study group and other specialists who read my earlier drafts in whole or in part. These included Robert Bradnock, David Taylor, Peter Lyon, Terry Byres, Gautem Sen, Tom Nossiter, Anita Inder Singh,

Bertram Farmer, Ian Anthony, Stephen Shenfield and Kate Grosser.

This book would not have been possible without the unstinting support of the staff of Chatham House. In particular, Chatham House Library and Press Library gave help way beyond the call of duty; Lesley Pitman and Jenny Foreman deserve special thanks. My thanks go also to Margaret May who worked meticulously to improve the text; to my Stakhanovite colleagues on the Soviet Foreign Policy Programme, Alex Pravda, Gerry Segal, Shyama Iyer, Sue Swasey, Robert Sasson and Jim Nichols; and to my mother, Lucy Duncan, for her forbearance while I was writing this.

Finally, I gratefully acknowledge the financial support of the Economic and Social Research Council (grant no. EOO 22 2011).

September 1988   P.D.

1

INTRODUCTION

This study is one of three Chatham House Papers dealing with Soviet relations with friendly Third World countries. These studies have sought to investigate the reasons for the close relations between the USSR and the country concerned, and the principal areas of difficulty between them; to examine the degree of influence exercised by the Soviet Union over the Third World country, and the leverage held by the latter over the former; and to attempt to assess the balance of costs and benefits to the USSR and its Third World partner in the relationship. The other two papers are *The Soviet Union and Cuba* by Peter Shearman (Routledge, 1987) and *The Soviet Union and Syria* by Efraim Karsh (Routledge, 1988). The purpose of this paper is to examine the Soviet-Indian relationship, focusing on the period from 1971 to the present.

The relationship between the Soviet Union and India is unique: India is the only non-communist developing country with which the Soviet Union has been able to maintain stable, friendly relations for a prolonged period – over three decades. On first impressions, it might appear surprising that it was India which should have had such a successful relationship with the Soviet Union. The country still suffers from a rigid caste system, despite the efforts of the government. Moreover, although India takes pride in being a secular state, it is one in which religion is of prime importance in the social life of most of the population. Both atheism and communism as philosophical ideas are rejected by the overwhelming majority of Indians. The country is a multi-party democracy with free trade

1

unions and a free press. It is culturally and economically closer to the West than to the USSR; English, the language of the former colonial master, remains an official language of the country and is widely used in business, the media and the more elitist educational institutions. All these factors might lead Indians generally, and Indian decision-makers in particular, to be suspicious of close links with the Soviet Union – and indeed might make Soviet decision-makers cautious in their dealings with India.

Western studies of the Soviet-Indian relationship have focused on the question of how much the Soviet Union has influenced, and been influenced by, India. Specialists have generally concluded that India's closeness to the Soviet Union on most foreign-policy issues arises from a coincidence of interests rather than from pressure or influence from one side or the other.[1] Some writers perceive India to be a client or an ally of the USSR. Henry Kissinger, the US Secretary of State under President Richard Nixon, for example, holds that the Indo-Soviet Treaty of Peace, Friendship and Cooperation, signed in 1971, 'was hard to reconcile with India's nonalignment'.[2] By contrast, a report prepared in 1985 by the Congressional Research Service for the House of Representatives Foreign Affairs Committee stated: 'India has succeeded in keeping its principles and interests in its relations with Moscow firmly intact.'[3] Here, I shall suggest that the word 'ally', and even more so 'client', conveys a greater degree of association than is justified by the reality of India's position in relation to the Soviet Union. The treaty is more than a non-aggression pact, since it requires the parties to consult in the event of an attack on one of them. But it is less than an alliance, since it does not require the parties to provide material support in the event of such an attack.

India and the USSR are friends. Neither has sacrificed any vital interests for the sake of the relationship. In general, neither can be said to depend on the other for the defence of its vital interests. An exception to this, perhaps, is found in the period of the Indo-Pakistan war of 1971 which led to the independence of Bangladesh. It is quite possible that if the Soviet Union had not acted in support of the Indians and East Bengalis, India would not have won the war. Its victory and the consequent break-up of Pakistan, however, made it the dominant power in South Asia, and reduced its need for Soviet support. Moscow, for its part, was not able to prevent New Delhi from seeking to improve its relations with Beijing and Washington, or from acquiring the capacity to make nuclear weapons. It was able to dissuade the Indians from voting against it over Afghanistan at the United Nations, but not (except for a brief period) to gain Indian support on the question. It was able to win India's support for its policies aimed at a world free of nuclear weapons; this was demonstrated during the visit of the General Secretary of the Central Committee of the Communist Party of the Soviet Union (CPSU), Mikhail Gorbachev, to New Delhi in November 1986. But it was unable, in 1986–8, to win support for a system of international security in Asia and the Pacific, put forward by Gorbachev in his speech of 28 July 1986 in Vladivostok, just as it had been unable to win India's support for General Secretary Leonid Brezhnev's plans for Asian collective security, first advanced in 1969. India, on the other hand, was able after the treaty to use its influence to prevent the USSR from selling arms to Pakistan, but unable, during eight years of quiet persuading, to prevail upon the Soviet Union to withdraw from Afghanistan, until other factors forced a change of mind in Moscow.

The importance of India to the Soviet Union
Several factors testify to the importance with which the Soviet Union regards India. Perhaps the most obvious and salient is the large number of high-level visits by top politicians, ministers, military leaders and trade officials to India. Brezhnev visited twice as General Secretary, in 1973 and 1980, and Gorbachev's first visit to any foreign country in Asia or the Third World was to India. It is the Soviet Union's largest Third World trading partner. Between 1964 and 1985 it was the largest non-communist recipient of Soviet aid. The Soviet government has supplied India with the latest in its military technology, on occasion even before its East European allies have been offered the chance to buy it. Another indication is the frequency with which Soviet commentators refer to Soviet-Indian relations as a model for ties between the USSR and non-socialist states.

The principal aim of the foreign policy of the Soviet Union, as of any country, is to seek to guarantee the security of the state. India's political and strategic importance arises from its geographical position, near to the southern frontier of the USSR and sharing borders with China and Pakistan. During the cold war, Moscow

3

wanted India to avoid participating in the *cordon sanitaire* established by the West around the Soviet bloc. India was seen as a friendly state, which might perhaps in the future provide naval or military bases, as well as acting as a counterweight to the presence of Pakistan in the American-led military alliance system. Whereas the United States encouraged countries to join Western security alliances, the aim of the USSR was merely to discourage them from doing this, rather than to persuade them to form alliances with itself. The purpose was to prevent territory or ocean from being used as a possible launching-point for attacks on the Soviet Union. Such an approach was more attractive to newly independent countries such as India, whose susceptibilities were offended by attempts to reincorporate them in military ties so soon after winning freedom.

At some point in the late 1950s, as the Sino-Soviet split developed (but before it emerged into the open), policy-makers in Moscow saw a friendly India as a possible counterweight to China. The Soviet Union sought to maintain good relations with both India and Pakistan for this purpose, but in 1971 it was forced to choose between the two. Pakistan by then had developed close relations with both the United States and China, so it is not surprising that the Soviet Union backed India. From that point on, India became its principal friend in Asia, and one of particular value when, at the end of the 1970s, the USA, Japan, China and Pakistan all appeared to be arrayed against the Soviet Union.

In addition, the geographical position of India, surrounded as it is by the Indian Ocean and close to the unstable Gulf region, gave it particular importance. After the Soviet invasion of Afghanistan, India was seen as a possible point of pressure on Pakistan. As Soviet relations with China improved in the 1980s, the position of India as a counterweight to China became less valuable to Moscow.

Beyond these geopolitical factors prompting Moscow to seek New Delhi's support in the Asian context, Soviet diplomacy has looked for Indian assistance in the broader, global context. India has considerable weight and prestige in international forums, and has the capacity to assist Soviet aims in the non-aligned movement (NAM), the United Nations General Assembly and the Commonwealth. In practice, India has followed its own perceptions of its interests in deciding whether to support particular Soviet policies. In some cases, where interests converge, as over American nuclear weapons programmes, apartheid or Kampuchea, India has backed

Soviet positions. In others, where India has been unhappy about Soviet actions, but has been unwilling, for other reasons, to antagonize its Soviet friends, it has muted its criticism. Examples include the Soviet invasion of Hungary in 1956 and of Afghanistan in 1979. In still other cases, where India has seen its interests threatened by Soviet-backed moves, it has not hesitated to oppose them. The outstanding instance here was the attempt by Cuba in the late 1970s and early 1980s to promote the idea that the 'socialist camp' was the 'natural ally' of the NAM. This was vigorously rejected by India, which saw it as a threat to the principles of non-alignment.

When India does share positions with the Soviet Union, however, this is of considerable political and ideological value to Moscow. At times in the 1970s and 1980s, the Soviet leaders must have felt alone in the world – not unlike the Bolsheviks after 1917 – with only their allies in the Council for Mutual Economic Assistance (CMEA) to back them up, instead of the whole working-class of Western Europe. In such conditions, the support of a significant non-socialist country – indeed, the largest non-socialist country in the world – is of considerable psychological importance. Moreover, from an ideological viewpoint, such support has its internal propaganda uses as well: the progressive policies of the Politburo have the backing of a major independent power. India's position can, furthermore, be relatively easily explained in terms of Lenin's writings about the anti-imperialist struggles of the peoples of the East, and this in itself gives strength to the ruling ideology.

Relations with India have economic benefits as well as costs. India is seen as a source of relatively inexpensive foods, raw materials, consumer goods and semi-manufactures which, owing to the rouble-rupee agreement, can be paid for in soft currency. Increasingly also, as the technological level of Indian industry has advanced, the country has become a source of more sophisticated products and services, of benefit to the Soviet economy and requiring only rupee expenditures. Furthermore, India is an outlet for Soviet-manufactured products which might be hard to sell in the increasingly competitive world market. It also absorbs the products of the Soviet defence industry, keeping production lines moving. Soviet economic relations with India, as well as Soviet development aid, have, over and above their economic purposes, an avowedly political aim. This is to reduce the dependence of India on the West and to enable it to pursue its own foreign policy and economic independence.

5

Naturally Moscow has hoped by such means to win India's friendship.

There is some dispute about whether, in the long run, the Kremlin would like to see a communist India. It is clear that the spread of communism has not always been a blessing to the Soviet Union: the experience of China under Mao, particularly the Cultural Revolution, has left bitter memories for Russians. Communist victories in Cuba and Vietnam, while providing considerable strategic gains, especially in the naval sphere, have also cost the Soviet Union dear in economic terms. If, however, one believes that among the members of the Politburo there are people who have been brought up on Marxist-Leninist precepts, who want to return to Leninist principles, and who believe that their system should be a model for the whole world (even if they are not sure about the exact nature of that system), then one cannot exclude the likelihood that the victory of communism in India is seen as a long-term goal. The point, however, is that it is such a very long-term goal that it falls off the list of Soviet foreign-policy priorities. Soviet specialists on India emphasize the lack of progress made in modernizing the political culture of what they rightly see as a highly traditional society.

For decades, Soviet aid has been concentrated on the state sector of the economy, which, at least for a time, was seen as a possible starting-point for socialism. Moscow has given some support to the Communist Party of India (CPI), and has recently improved its relations with the breakaway Communist Party of India (Marxist) (CPI[M]). Although in the 1984 general elections the CPI(M) became the largest single national opposition party in the Lok Sabha (lower house of parliament), both CPs together have never risen to 10% of the vote. The Soviet leaders have considered it more profitable to give their backing to the Congress (I) Party of Indira Gandhi and Rajiv Gandhi, since it is the party in power and usually pursues policies which are compatible with Soviet interests. When the CPI has followed Moscow's urgings and given backing to the Congress (I) Party's foreign policies, and even to its domestic policies, it has lost votes. The (natural) pursuit by Moscow of Soviet state interests at the expense of Indian communists has been a cause of discord within the CPI and between the CPI and Moscow. The principal aim of the Soviet propaganda machine, which makes considerable efforts in India, is to promote a positive image of the USSR as a country rather than of communism as such (although the two are naturally linked). This effort is aimed at the public at large, and particularly at the intelligentsia, the press, business, the Administrative Service, diplomats and politicians.

A brief explanation may be in order here about the institutions and individuals involved in the making of Soviet policy towards India. The principal institutions concerned have been the Politburo of the Central Committee of the CPSU, the Council of Ministers, the Ministry of Foreign Affairs and the Ministry of Defence. By 1971, the locus of initiative in foreign policy had shifted decisively to the General Secretary, Leonid Brezhnev, with the Prime Minister, Aleksei Kosygin, having a secondary role. This pattern has lasted up to the present, with the Prime Minister, currently Nikolai Ryzhkov, having a particular role in economic relations, although he is not limited to this field. The primary role of Deputy Prime Ministers is normally an economic one.

The key position of the Minister of Foreign Affairs in policy-making was symbolized by the promotion of the veteran Foreign Minister Andrei Gromyko to be a full Politburo member in 1973, and the promotion of Eduard Shevardnadze in 1985 to similar Politburo status immediately before he succeeded Gromyko as Foreign Minister. Within the ministry, a First Deputy Minister (currently Iuly Vorontsov, who was ambassador to India 1977–83) has supervised a Deputy Minister responsible for Asia (currently Igor Rogachev), who in turn supervises the South Asian Countries Administration which is responsible for India. The Ministry of Foreign Affairs deals with security and economic relations. The Ministry of Defence, in its dealings with India, is concerned mainly with arms transfers, as well as any other forms of military cooperation. After 1986, the International Department of the Central Committee played an enhanced role in the formation of Soviet foreign policy, under Anatoly Dobrynin. Before then, the International Department, as far as can be seen, was concerned mainly with relations with the communist parties in India. After Dobrynin took over, however, he began to be listed in meetings with Indian governmental delegations. He retired in September 1988 and the radical reformer Aleksandr Iakovlev took control of a new committee to deal with international affairs. The South Asia sector of the department has been headed by Pyotr Kotsubin since at least 1982.

A number of economic institutions are involved in working out the details of trade with India. They include the Ministry of Foreign

Trade and the State Committee for External Economic Links (formerly the State Committee for Economic Links). Since the decentralization of foreign trade planning, introduced in 1987, a wider range of bodies has become involved. Cultural links are controlled by the Ministry of Culture. The research institutes of the Academy of Sciences, particularly the Institute of World Economics and International Relations (IMEMO) and the Institute of Oriental Studies (IOS), play an advisory role. What influence the KGB exerts is obscure but doubtless important. Little research has been done on the influence of the Foreign Affairs Commissions of the USSR Supreme Soviet (both headed by Central Committee Secretaries), so their role, too, is uncertain.

The aims of Indian foreign policy
It is not possible in the framework of this book to provide a thorough analysis of Indian foreign policy. Here I can only outline its aims as they relate to India's links with the Soviet Union.

The overriding aim has been to assure the internal and external security of India. Since independence, India's overwhelming pre-occupation in foreign policy has been with Pakistan. The lasting effect of the partition of British India has been not so much to raise questions over whether to accept partition, as to leave a legacy of suspicion and fear in India of Pakistan, and in Pakistan of India. Both countries claim the state of Jammu and Kashmir, which after the post-independence war was occupied partly by Pakistan ('Azad Kashmir', or 'Pakistan-occupied Kashmir') and partly by India. The 1965 and 1971 wars between the two countries helped to confirm the 'enemy image' of Pakistan in India. Further anxieties were created in India by Islamabad's relations with the United States and China, both of which assisted the rearmament of Pakistan; by Pakistan's development of nuclear weapons; and by its support for, or at least tolerance of, terrorist groups operating in India, in particular Sikh extremists. The fact that for most of its history Pakistan has been ruled by the military, and has frequently appeared to be unstable, has added to India's fears.

The second major perceived threat to India's security has been China. Although the two countries have not fought a war since 1962, border tension has occurred periodically. The demarcation of much of the 2,500-mile frontier remains disputed. Even though a full-scale

Chinese invasion of India across the Himalayas is seen as highly unlikely, the size and firepower of the People's Liberation Army is substantially greater than that of the Indian armed forces. Anxiety in India was increased by the development of Chinese nuclear weapons and by the rehabilitation of China, in American eyes, under President Nixon, since this reduced the possibility of an American nuclear umbrella for India against an attack from China. This anxiety led Mrs Gandhi to order research which culminated in India's acquisition of a nuclear weapons capability. Additional problems for India have been Chinese backing for the Naga and Assamese rebels in the north-east of India, and China's attempts to increase its influence in Nepal. Perhaps the main problem (apart from the border itself) is China's 30-year-old support for Pakistan. It has transferred arms worth over \$2 billion to Pakistan since the mid-1960s. The Karakoram highway, completed in 1978 and running from China through Pakistan-controlled Kashmir into Pakistan, provides an important strategic link for both countries. However, since the re-establishment of diplomatic relations between China and India in 1976, and efforts on both sides to improve links, China has been seen as less of a threat in India.

Pakistani support for the Sikh terrorists, Chinese support for Naga and Mizo rebels, and links between the Tamils in Sri Lanka and South India highlight the link between the internal security of India and its foreign policy. In general, India seeks to enhance its security by having good relations with all its smaller neighbours in South Asia. At the same time, its superiority in territory, population size and economic development lead it to expect to be the dominant South Asian power. The disparity in size between India and its neighbours in South Asia, together with memories of occasions when India has asserted itself against them, such as the 1975 annexation of Sikkim or the 1987 intervention in Sri Lanka, tend to alarm India's neighbours and complicate their relations with India. The fact that India is a democracy which is tolerant of diverse national, linguistic and religious groups also poses a certain ideological threat to its neighbours. Only Sri Lanka, among India's neighbours, has maintained a democratic system.

Faced with the perceived threats to its security from Pakistan and China, India has responded by trying to reduce the level of outside support for these countries. It was initially American support for Pakistan that encouraged India to seek Soviet assistance as a counterweight. Later Chinese support for Pakistan reinforced India's links with the USSR. India has sought and gained Soviet backing in diplomatic forums, particularly at the United Nations, over its conflicts with Pakistan. During the 1971 war the Soviet navy deployed its ships to deter American naval moves against India in the Bay of Bengal. The main continuing Soviet security support to India is in the form of arms transfers. Between 60% and 70% of all India's arms imports come from the USSR. These come more cheaply than their rival products from the West, with easier credit terms. Additionally, the Soviet Union has helped India towards achieving its objective of an independent arms industry.

While pursuing its friendship with Moscow, India has continued to defend its independence and the principles of non-alignment. When the Indian Prime Minister, Jawaharlal Nehru, together with Tito, Nasser and other leaders, developed the principles of non-alignment in the 1950s, they did not equate non-alignment with neutrality or equidistance between the two major military blocs. The ideas of anti-colonialism, anti-imperialism, equality of states and non-interference in the internal affairs of other states led India, more often than not, to back the Soviet rather than the American side, if only because America's capacity for global involvement was greater than that of the Soviet Union. Perhaps the key to India's conception of non-alignment is not only its refusal to join any military alliance, but also its denial to any foreign power of military or naval bases. It would like to keep the superpowers and China out of South Asia, and out of the Indian Ocean. Without external involvement, India would be in a position to dominate the subcontinent and the surrounding waters (leaving aside the problems related to the Pakistani nuclear bomb). It perceives outside involvement as tending to complicate and aggravate situations which should be resolved between neighbours. When other countries bring in outside powers, however, India believes it has to respond by also seeking outside help. Since the time of Nehru, pragmatism has been a necessary part of non-alignment.

At the same time India, like other non-aligned states, has sought good relations with both East and West, with the aims of improving its security and maximizing its opportunities for economic development. In the 1950s, when India was attempting to develop heavy industry, it encountered resistance from Western countries which thought it should concentrate on its traditional products. There were also objections to its desire to expand the state sector. It was then that the Soviet Union stepped in and built a steel mill at Bhilai – the first major Soviet aid project in India. Since then the willingness of the Soviet Union to provide development aid has encouraged Western countries and aid agencies to compete, with regard to both the types of projects they will finance and the terms involved. Although the Soviet share of aid to India is not substantial, it is seen as important in New Delhi because of its effect on the West, and because it has been aimed at boosting India's basic productive industries, such as steel and power; similarly, the fact that New Delhi has persuaded Moscow of India's importance, ensuring it first place among non-communist recipients of Soviet aid, is a cause for gratification in India.

India has played a leading role among the less developed countries (LDCs) in articulating their demand for a New International Economic Order. This aims, among other things, at forcing Western countries to open up their markets to LDC competition, increasing the prices paid for primary products and reducing the interest rates on Third World debt. While the USA, the EC countries and Japan have tended to resist such proposals, the Soviet Union has regularly spoken of the justice of Third World attempts to overcome the legacy of Western imperialism.

The main aim of India's trading policy is to secure resources for development, from wherever it can get them. American reluctance to supply India with the latest technology causes problems in Indo-American relations. It leads India to respond in apparently contradictory ways: to make efforts to persuade the Americans of its reliability and desire for friendship; and to seek what technology it can from other sources, be they Western, Japanese, Chinese or Soviet. The USSR has proclaimed its willingness to provide India with whatever technology it is capable of absorbing. India benefits from the Soviet trading pattern, since this allows access to Soviet goods and technology without the expenditure of hard currency. It also allows guaranteed access to the Soviet market for Indian products.

Facets of the relationship

The key to the success of the Soviet-Indian relationship is geopolitical. The two countries lack a common border, but do have common enemies or adversaries. China, which during the 1970s and early 1980s was an adversary of the Soviet Union, was allied with Pakistan, the traditional enemy of India. Moreover, India and China were neighbours with a history of hostility. The fourth side of the quadrilateral – the relationship between the USSR and Pakistan – did not become one of direct conflict until after the April 1978 revolution in Afghanistan. A further complicating factor is the position of the USA – on the China-Pakistan side in 1971, with ups and downs thereafter, but playing an important role in Pakistan from 1981.

The global aspects of the relationship flow from the Asian, geopolitical aspects. Subject to their own interests, the Soviet Union and India support each other's position in East-West and North-South competition, and in international political forums. The economic and defence facets of the relationship are intertwined, since India pays for its arms purchases by supplying the Soviet Union with goods. These exchanges involve gains and losses for Moscow, but India has probably gained more than the Soviet Union. It is in this economic-defence relationship that the Soviet Union has paid a price, in order to maintain India's friendship in both the Asian and the global context. Moscow also conducts propaganda efforts aimed at Indian opinion, publicizing its assistance to India both past and present.

Despite the importance of these facets of the relationship, the ideological aspects should not be neglected. Nehru's Fabian socialism and a degree of sympathy for the Soviet experiment were shared by many in the succeeding generation of the Indian elite, some of whom are even now in influential positions. It was not pure rhetoric when Prime Minister Rajiv Gandhi said at the banquet for Gorbachev in New Delhi on 25 November 1986:

There must be something deeper than mutual gain to explain the endurance and vitality of this [Soviet-Indian] friendship. Indeed there is. It is our abhorrence of imperialism, our struggle against colonialism and racism. It is our shared commitment to the principles of human equality and social justice. These principles transcend the differences in our historical background and in the political and social systems built by Lenin in your country and by Mahatma Gandhi and Jawaharlal Nehru in ours.[4]

In this study, I examine the historical development of the bilateral Soviet-Indian relationship (Chapter 2). Following this, I look at the geopolitical basis of the ties between the two countries in their Asian context (Chapter 3) and the wider, global aspects of the relationship (Chapter 4). The economic and defence side is then considered (Chapter 5). Next I outline the underlying Soviet approaches to India and Indian foreign policy, seeking to illuminate the Soviet policies detailed earlier (Chapter 6), and examine Soviet attempts to popularize their policies and image within India itself (Chapter 7). In conclusion, I attempt to weigh up the gains and losses to the Soviet Union and India in the relationship; and I discuss the future of Soviet-Indian ties and some implications for Britain and the West (Chapter 8).

Possible sources of change in the relationship appear on both the Soviet and Indian sides. The 'new political thinking' promoted by the Gorbachev leadership might affect the Soviet-Indian relationship in several ways. The strenuous efforts to improve Moscow's relations with Beijing and the attempts to reach a settlement in Afghanistan with Islamabad could both have unfavourable consequences for India. Further, the Soviet Union seems less willing than before to overextend itself in the Third World, although this may affect the countries of 'socialist orientation' rather than those maintaining mixed economies. Indeed, it seems that Gorbachev favours extending Soviet ties with large, non-socialist Third World countries, from Mexico and Brazil to Saudi Arabia. The Soviet-Indian relationship is a model for this type of link.[5] On the Indian side, there is also a new generation in the leadership; in addition, India's economic needs are encouraging it to look westward for the latest technology. I shall suggest that, in this changing environment, both sides consider that they have benefited from the relationship and that a significant change is unlikely.

Two caveats should be noted at once. Although this is a study in Soviet foreign policy, it would be quite wrong to present the Soviet Union as the sole actor in the relationship with India, or indeed with any other country. To do so might give the impression that Moscow makes decisions and the rest of the world follows. In the context of Asia, the reverse is rather the case. For most of the period since 1971, at least, Moscow was reacting to events in South Asia rather than shaping them. It follows that considerable attention must be given to the policies of India and its neighbours. A second danger follows from the fact that, at least until recently, much more information about the relationship has come out of New Delhi than out of Moscow. There is therefore a natural temptation to focus on the Indian side of the link. Concentration on Soviet sources, on the other hand, can be misleading about the actions of the USSR. It is essential to collect evidence from both sides, and also from other countries affected by the relationship.

2
THE BILATERAL RELATIONSHIP

Historical background

Most Indian and Soviet accounts of the history of relations between the two countries begin by referring to the migration to India of the Aryans four thousand years ago from what is now Soviet Central Asia. The Russian merchant Afanasy Nikitin visited northern India in the fifteenth century and published an account of his travels. In the seventeenth century, Indian traders settled in Astrakhan, from where they sent goods to Moscow and later to St Petersburg. Contacts became more frequent from the end of the eighteenth century. In the nineteenth century, the Russian and British empires clashed, as the British push from India into Afghanistan collided with the Russian drive south. After the failure of the Indian Mutiny in 1857, some of the rebels took refuge in Russia. In 1885 the Russian Orientalist Ivan Minaev attended the founding meeting of the Indian National Congress in Bombay. Mohandas Gandhi's commitment to non-violence was heavily influenced by his reading of the works of Lev Tolstoy, with whom he corresponded.

The October Revolution and the anti-colonialist appeals of the Bolshevik leaders gave a boost to Indian nationalism. In 1928, after visiting the USSR, the future Indian Prime Minister, Jawaharlal Nehru, wrote that the British in India had used 'the bogy of a Russian invasion' to encourage Indian hostility to first Tsarist and then Soviet Russia.[1]

Nehru was sympathetic to the Soviet Union and admired its rapid industrial progress under central planning. In the first years of Indian independence after 1947, the Soviet leadership did not reciprocate the friendly feelings that Nehru had for the USSR. Stalin initially saw the Nehru government as compromising with British imperialism. Before Stalin's death, however, the Soviet Union began to show a more friendly attitude. In the mid-1950s, Moscow's favourable reassessment of nationalist governments laid the basis for good Soviet-Indian relations. In 1955, the Soviet Union agreed to build for the Indian government a steel mill at Bhilai (in Madhya Pradesh) with a capacity of one million tons, after negotiations with firms from Britain and the FRG had dragged on. An important milestone was the visit to India of the Soviet leaders Nikita Khrushchev and Nikolai Bulganin in December of that year. This visit convinced Khrushchev that Nehru's Congress Party, with its mass support, was a more useful instrument for the promotion of Soviet interests than the CPI. Since then, the Soviet leaders have made friendship with Indian governments a priority, at first by rendering valuable support to India in the United Nations over Kashmir and Goa. Such fluctuations in the relationship as there have been have usually originated on the Indian side.

It is difficult to determine at what point the desire for a counter-weight to China became a major factor in Soviet policy towards India. According to T.N. Kaul (later the Indian ambassador in Moscow, and a Soviet favourite), Khrushchev told the Indian Vice-President, S. Radhakrishnan, in 1956 that 'in ten years' time the chief enemy [of the Soviet Union] would be China'.[2] In 1958, Khrushchev proposed a summit conference on the Middle East, with the inclusion of India but not of China. In 1959, the border clashes between India and China led to Soviet calls for talks and to reaffirmations of Soviet friendship with both sides. This neutral position pleased the Indians but stung the Chinese. In 1960, for the first time, India bought arms from the Soviet Union – helicopters and planes, for possible use against China. In 1962, the military relationship went further, when the Soviet government agreed to allow India to produce MiG-21 aircraft under licence, although it had supplied only MiG-19s to China. This did not prevent the Soviet leaders from initially backing China in the Sino-Indian war of autumn 1962, when they needed Chinese support in the Cuban missile crisis. After this crisis was defused, the Soviet leaders switched back to a policy of cordiality with Nehru, and *Pravda* expressed the Soviet desire to maintain friendship with both sides.

In May 1964 Nehru died and was succeeded by L.B. Shastri. In October Brezhnev and Kosygin took over from the deposed Khrushchev. Almost at the same time, China exploded its first atomic bomb. Perceiving India as weakened by the war with China two years earlier, the new Soviet leaders sought to improve their relations with Pakistan, and to try to wean it away from China. Thus, in the 1965 clashes between India and Pakistan, which erupted into full-scale war in August, Moscow stayed officially neutral, although it continued to supply arms to India. The United States declared an arms embargo, which affected Pakistan much more adversely than India. It was from about this time that the USSR became a major exporter of arms to India, while China supported Pakistan. The restraint adopted by the Soviet Union meant that after the belligerents had fought to a stalemate, Moscow was acceptable to both sides as a mediator. Washington, like Moscow, desiring to unite India and Pakistan against China, encouraged Kosygin to play this role. The Tashkent conference of January 1966 was a considerable success for the Soviet role in South Asia. It allowed Moscow to maintain good relations with both India and Pakistan until the end of the 1960s.

After Shastri's death at Tashkent, Indira Gandhi succeeded as Prime Minister. Her friendliness to the United States alarmed the Soviet leaders. Between 1966 and 1968 the Soviet Union increased its economic aid to Pakistan and also sold it helicopters and other arms. Kosygin visited New Delhi in January 1968 to assure Mrs Gandhi of the Soviet commitment to India, but despite Indian pressure it emerged in July that the USSR had made an arms deal with Pakistan. The Indian response was to express 'regret' over the Soviet invasion of Czechoslovakia and to abstain in the Security Council (as, incidentally, Pakistan did as well); more importantly, Mrs Gandhi sought to improve relations with China. Sino-Soviet relations were at a low point at this time. In March 1969 there were clashes on the Ussuri river, and in June Brezhnev put forward proposals for a collective security system in Asia. This scheme aimed at 'containing' China by associating the surrounding states, including both India and Pakistan. By this time, Moscow may have begun to fear the possibility of close relations between Washington and Beijing.

The friendship treaty and the Indo-Pakistani war of 1971
Meanwhile, India continued to emphasize to Moscow that Soviet arms sales to Pakistan could only harm Soviet-Indian relations. In effect, India was forcing Moscow to choose between it and Pakistan. Some time during the second half of 1968, Soviet diplomats told their Indian counterparts that India mattered much more than Pakistan to the USSR, and that if India wished to have a formal treaty with the Soviet Union, the latter would oblige at any time.[3] During 1969, Pakistan's relations with China were consolidated, whereas those with the USSR deteriorated. In May 1969, Kosygin visited India for President Zakir Husain's funeral. During his visit Mrs Gandhi held meetings with Kosygin in which no other Indians were present (only Soviet interpreters were used), and Nihal Singh suggests that an Indo-Soviet treaty was discussed. Possibly Indira Gandhi, being aware of the approaching clash with the right wing of Congress, thought that the treaty would bolster her left-leaning image.[4] According to T.N. Kaul, who at that time was Indian Foreign Secretary (the most senior civil servant in the ministry), it was not until the end of 1970 that a draft treaty was agreed between the Soviet and Indian sides, after discussions which had lasted for about two years. A Soviet source asserts that the USSR offered India a draft treaty in 1969. The Ministry of External Affairs examined it and concluded that it was not a military pact and did not violate Indian non-alignment. Work on the treaty was complete by the end of 1970. Kaul says that the negotiations were held in conditions of tight secrecy, with 'hardly half-a-dozen people' on the Indian side being aware of them. But even after the treaty had been agreed in draft form between the two sides, it could not yet be signed, because (according to Kaul) it was not easy to be sure of getting agreement for this in India. In his words, 'the main question, however, was how and when to persuade our government to sign it.' Kaul's account makes it clear that the crisis in the summer of 1971 provided the opportunity for the treaty to be made acceptable.[5]

Simultaneously, Indira Gandhi moved sharply to the left in her domestic policy by nationalizing fourteen major banks and forcing out of office Morarji Desai, the leader of the Congress right wing.

18

She won Soviet approval, and support from the CPI. This was important because opposition now to Indira Gandhi from the Congress right made her dependent for her Lok Sabha majority on the Communists. The Congress right split formally in November 1969. According to Nihal Singh, in September 1969 Foreign Minister Dinesh Singh went to Moscow and agreed the text of the treaty with the Soviet leaders. In view of Mrs Gandhi's problem within the Congress Party, Dinesh Singh explained that it would be inopportune to sign the treaty at that time, and the Soviet side accepted this. Moreover, Moscow agreed to avoid more commitments of arms sales to Pakistan. Despite Soviet willingness to accommodate her, the Indian Prime Minister refused to commit herself to Brezhnev's Asian collective security system, although her Foreign Minister had expressed support.[6]

In the March 1971 general election, Indira Gandhi won a landslide victory on a left-wing programme. Moscow supported her campaign and urged her to move further to the left. As Brezhnev commented in the Central Committee report to the 24th Congress of the CPSU in March 1971: 'In some countries progressive forces have already scored serious gains. One may merely recall, for instance, events like the recent nationalization of the big banks in India, and the impressive victory scored over the Right-wing forces at the last elections to the House of the People of the Indian Parliament.'[7]

Meanwhile, the Pakistani military government of Yahya Khan unleashed a wave of violent repression in East Bengal (East Pakistan), which had voted overwhelmingly for the party favouring autonomy for the province. The bloodshed in East Pakistan and the outflow of millions of refugees into India put pressure on New Delhi to use armed force in support of the Bengali resistance to the Islamabad government. While opinion in India and indeed in the West began to favour the independence of East Bengal, the USSR seems still to have wished to preserve its influence in a united Pakistan. It urged both Indira Gandhi and Yahya Khan to avoid the use of force in East Pakistan. This Soviet position could not be satisfactory to India. New Delhi was further worried in mid-July when Nixon announced that Henry Kissinger, his National Security Adviser, had secretly visited Beijing to arrange Nixon's visit there the following year. India's alarm was all the greater since it was Pakistan which had facilitated Kissinger's visit. The prospect of Pakistan getting support against India from not only China but also the United States was disturbing, especially in view of the Soviets' unwillingness to back India's position against Pakistan. Mrs Gandhi reacted by making friendly gestures towards China. This may have been a serious attempt to win Chinese neutrality over the future of East Pakistan; it certainly was intended to present Moscow with the possibility of improved Sino-Indian relations. In any event, there seems to have been little response from Beijing.

The government of India now decided that the time was ripe to sign the friendship treaty with Moscow. On 8 August Soviet Foreign Minister Gromyko arrived in New Delhi. Within a day the 'Indo-Soviet Treaty of Peace, Friendship and Cooperation' was announced. The most significant section from the viewpoint of India's interests was Article IX: 'Each High Contracting Party undertakes to abstain from providing any assistance to any third party that engages in armed conflict with [the] other Party. In the event of either Party being subjected to an attack or a threat thereof, the High Contracting Parties shall immediately enter into mutual consultations in order to remove any such threat and to take appropriate effective measures to ensure peace and the security of their countries.' In the prevailing situation it prevented the Soviet Union from sending arms to Pakistan; and it obliged Moscow to help New Delhi settle the East Bengal question. The treaty did not constitute a formal alliance. Although it stated that 'India respects the peace-loving policy' of the USSR, it also declared, as a quid pro quo, that the Soviet Union 'respects India's policy of non-alignment' (Article IV). Moreover, Article VIII precluded the two countries from participating in 'any military alliance directed against the other Party'. Article X reaffirmed this point and specifically ruled out secret alliances. This may have been intended to remove Soviet fears that India might come to an understanding with China against the USSR.[8] Indeed, from a Soviet viewpoint, the treaty was probably understood as part of the planned network of bilateral treaties which would underpin Brezhnev's Asian collective security project, and which was designed to isolate China. India's interests were more immediate: to deter China and the United States from intervening to help Yahya Khan (a motivation which would hold true even if, as has been suggested, India believed that China had told Pakistan it would not intervene in an Indo-Pakistani war); to ensure Soviet diplomatic support, especially at the United Nations; and to prevent Moscow from supplying arms to Pakistan. The summer of 1971 provided the conditions in which the treaty could now be presented attractively to the public. It was welcomed by all parties in the Lok Sabha apart from the Swatantra. India now had support from a friend.

Henry Kissinger has argued that Moscow was encouraging India to attack Pakistan, claiming that 'the Soviet Union played a highly inflammatory role', and that Moscow desired the defeat of Pakistan, since it would be a blow to the American network of alliances and would 'demonstrate Chinese impotence'.[9] But even after the signing of the treaty, Moscow continued publicly to call for a political settlement of the crisis in East Bengal. Brezhnev, Kosygin and President Nikolai Podgorny all met Indira Gandhi in Moscow on 28 September, and seem to have tried to use the treaty as a brake on India's drift towards war. Kosygin urged India to avoid the military instrument. Robert Donaldson and Robert Horn both see Soviet diplomacy as playing a restraining role in India, right up to the end of October, when Moscow began to express full support for India's policies. Throughout November the Kremlin continued to send arms to India for use against Pakistan. On 3 December, Pakistan attacked Indian airfields, provoking India to launch an all-out attack on the Pakistani forces in East Bengal. Between then and the Pakistani surrender on 16 December, the Soviet Union helped India in several ways. It warned China not to intervene in support of Pakistan (possibly threatening diversionary activity in Sinkiang). It deployed naval forces to deter the American ships which had been sent to the Bay of Bengal. In the UN Security Council, it vetoed three American-backed resolutions which sought a cease-fire and the withdrawal of Indian troops. Kissinger claims that he and Nixon were trying to preserve the independence of the Western rump of Pakistan, which they believed India wished to end. Nihal Singh seems right to assert that neither Moscow nor New Delhi wanted West Pakistan to disintegrate, and indeed Kissinger himself suggests that it was Soviet pressure which persuaded Indira Gandhi to offer a cease-fire.[10]

Moscow and Mrs Gandhi, 1971–7
The USSR had helped India in defeating Pakistan against the combined opposition of the USA and China, and Soviet prestige in India rose to new heights. Soviet influence on Indian policy-making,

21

however, did not increase. This was because India was in a sufficiently strong position after its victory not to have to rely on Soviet support. Mrs Gandhi was sensitive to charges that the treaty and her relations with Moscow were a deviation from non-alignment, and generally downplayed the treaty. For example, she said in 1973: 'It is just a friendship treaty; it does not affect our policy.'[11] Whereas in 1971 it was Moscow that had emphasized the economic and political sides of the treaty and India that had stressed the defence side, after the Bangladesh war the roles were reversed.

In November 1973 Brezhnev and Gromyko visited New Delhi. This was Brezhnev's first foreign trip to an Asian state since becoming General Secretary. It was an important publicity exercise for Soviet-Indian friendship, played up by the Soviet media and to a lesser extent by the Indian media as well. Brezhnev promoted his scheme for an Asian collective security system, but Mrs Gandhi was unresponsive and the concept was omitted from the final communiqué. Several economic agreements were signed, including one between Gosplan (the Soviet State Planning Commission) and the Indian Planning Commission on planning cooperation, and a fifteen-year trade agreement. It was at this summit that Indira Gandhi gave both warning and thanks to Brezhnev. 'In all these years, Soviet leaders have never put pressure on us, never dictated conditions to us, never imposed their will on us.'[12] Both leaders, in their speeches, referred to the treaty, although Brezhnev put more emphasis on it. A feature of Mrs Gandhi's speech was her reference to the Indian transition to socialism and to the Soviet role in this. 'After the dawn of freedom you were the first to help us in establishing gigantic industrial enterprises in the public sector, and thus began the strengthening of our relationship at another level. And that is how the meek, mute, down-trodden India of yesterday is today marching ahead along the path of progress, the path of socialism.' Brezhnev avoided the use of the term 'socialist' to describe Mrs Gandhi's policies, and emphasized the importance of Soviet-Indian relations as an example of uniting 'states with different social systems'. The furthest he would go to express agreement with Mrs Gandhi was to say, 'If now in India people talk about development in the direction of socialism, this, we understand, is the result of the historical experience of your country.' But he praised 'our esteemed friend', Indira Gandhi, for her role in forming 'India's progressive policy', leaving ambiguous whether the reference included domestic policy.[13]

The news of the Indian underground explosion of a 'nuclear device' at Pokharan, Rajasthan, in May 1974 was not well received in the USSR. Although described as a 'peaceful' nuclear explosion (PNE), it was a signal that India was now capable of producing nuclear weapons. As one of the states possessing nuclear weapons which was a also signatory to the nuclear Non-Proliferation Treaty (NPT), along with the USA and the UK, the Soviet Union was in principle opposed to diffusion of nuclear weapons. It was also concerned about the consequences of India's action for stability in the region. Publicly, however, the Soviet media repeated India's phrases about peaceful purposes, and also drew attention to the Chinese nuclear capability.

The Soviet Union fully supported Mrs Gandhi's actions during the 'emergency' of 1975–7, when she had large numbers of opposition leaders and trade unionists jailed. It backed her line that she was fighting a progressive battle against reactionaries, and specifically endorsed her '20-point programme' for socio-economic development. At the 25th Congress of the CPSU in February 1976, Brezhnev gave unprecedented praise to Indira Gandhi.

> To begin with, a few words about our many-sided co-operation with *India*. We attach special importance to friendship with that great country. In the past five years Soviet-Indian relations have risen to a new level. Our countries have concluded a treaty of peace, friendship and co-operation. And even this short period has clearly shown its tremendous significance for our bilateral ties, and its role as a stabilizing factor in South Asia and the continent as a whole.
>
> Close political and economic co-operation with the Republic of India is our constant policy. Soviet people appreciate and, more, are in solidarity with India's peace-loving foreign policy and the courageous efforts of her progressive forces to solve the country's difficult socio-economic problems. We wish the people and government of India complete success in these efforts.[14]

The CPI decided to follow Moscow's urgings and support Mrs Gandhi, although it asked that trade unions be allowed to function normally and criticized the 'misuse' of emergency powers against the people. The repression of the CPI(M) was not unwelcome to Moscow or the CPI. A feature of the emergency was the rise to prominence of Sanjay Gandhi, the Prime Minister's son and heir-apparent. Sanjay's attacks on the CPI, which before the end of the emergency won his mother's support, alarmed the pro-Moscow party but do not seem to have elicited any public opposition from Soviet officials.

In August 1975 a coup in Bangladesh replaced the government friendly to India and the Soviet Union with one more friendly to Pakistan and China. In the following April, India announced that it was restoring full diplomatic relations with China, and the next month it did likewise with Pakistan. The Sino-Indian rapprochement may have helped to encourage Moscow to be more generous to India with trade and arms. In June 1976, for the first time since 1971, Mrs Gandhi visited Moscow to reassure the Kremlin about Sino-Indian relations and to try to improve Indo-Soviet economic links. Although she still refused to endorse the Asian collective security system, Brezhnev reaffirmed Moscow's support for her internal policies. In December 1976, for the first time, the Soviet Union agreed to sell some of its much needed crude oil to India, and also to sell heavy water for India's Rajasthan reactor.

Moscow and the Janata government, 1977–80
When Indira Gandhi announced that elections would be held in March 1977, the Soviet media continued to give full backing to her Congress Party. Moscow denounced the anti-Indira Gandhi opposition, united under the 'Janata' label, as a representative of big landowners, monopolies and foreign interests. Morarji Desai, the Janata leader, was denounced as a CIA agent. What upset the Kremlin most was Janata's criticism of Mrs Gandhi for, in its view, deviating from non-alignment by tilting too far towards the Soviet Union. Desai promised 'genuine non-alignment' and threatened that the Indo-Soviet treaty might 'automatically go' if Janata won.[15] The CPI had an electoral pact with Congress and shared in its defeat. Its next moves were to break with Mrs Gandhi and to seek an alliance with the CPI(M). The clear victory of the Janata coalition was a blow to Moscow and presented the Indo-Soviet relationship with its severest test yet.

Moscow reacted by stopping all attacks on the Janata leaders. Indeed, Soviet commentators began to republish CPI criticism of anti-democratic moves undertaken during the emergency and to attribute Mrs Gandhi's defeat to these. The willingness of Soviet analysts to eat their words so quickly demonstrates the importance the leadership attached to good relations with India. A month after the election, Gromyko arrived in New Delhi, where he met Desai and his Foreign Minister, A.B. Vajpayee. The Soviet Foreign Minister expressed the desire to promote friendship and cooperation with India. Vajpayee responded by saying 'that the bonds of friendship between the two countries were strong enough to survive the demands of divergent systems, the fate of an individual or the fortunes of a political party.'[16] Inder K. Gujral, Indian ambassador in Moscow from May 1976 to November 1980, makes clear that this line was preserved in practice. 'On the basis of personal knowledge I can testify that Indo-Soviet relations during the Janata days were kept at a very even keel and there were many new additions to the areas of cooperation.'[17] The modification in the Janata attitude was almost as striking as the Soviet turnaround. Part of the explanation may be that, before coming to power, the Janata leaders had feared that the 1971 treaty contained some secret sections, but their concern had turned out to be baseless. What seems incontestable is that on reviewing the geopolitical environment of India from the perspective of government, they decided that the Soviet link had proved its worth. Vajpayee enthused about Soviet-Indian friendship and spoke of the need to raise the relationship to a new level. This view was welcomed by Gromyko's team, and three new economic agreements were signed. One of these involved a new 20-year credit, on the most favourable terms ever offered by Moscow to New Delhi, replacing existing credits which had not been fully taken up. This showed Moscow's willingness to pay a higher price for India's friendship as the need arose.

In October Desai and Vajpayee visited Moscow. The fact that Desai had been invited to Washington but had chosen to go first to Moscow showed the priority he gave to relations with the Soviet Union. Nevertheless, the Janata government took pains to reject any idea of a 'special relationship' between India and the Soviet Union. The joint communiqué issued after Desai's visit was rather warmer than that after Gromyko's visit to New Delhi (mentioning Indo-Soviet friendship as well as cooperation). It noted that 'Soviet-Indian friendship has survived the test of time', and added that it was 'an important factor in the cause of peace and stability in Asia and the whole world'.[18] This was the nearest reference to Brezhnev's Asian collective security system. Brezhnev and Desai failed to resolve a major issue in economic relations: the Soviet desire for compensation for the decline in the world value of the rupee. Agreement was reached on this only in late 1978, on terms favourable to India.

The Janata government wanted to improve relations with its South Asian neighbours, and also with the United States and China. In this it was following the stated policies of Indira Gandhi. President Jimmy Carter pleased India by blocking the sale of A-7 aircraft to Pakistan. He visited New Delhi in January 1978 and praised Desai for returning to a non-aligned position. China, too, became more friendly. When Vajpayee visited Moscow in September, he was treated to a barrage of anti-Chinese propaganda. At this time the Politburo was feeling particularly isolated in international politics, for Zbigniew Brzezinski, President Carter's National Security Adviser, was promoting what would effectively be a strategic alliance between the United States, China and Japan, directed against the Soviet Union. Vajpayee's visit to Beijing in February 1979 was the first by an Indian minister since 1962. In spite of opposition to this from Congress (I) and from within Janata, progress was made. The Chinese assured Vajpayee that they had ceased to aid the Naga and Mizo rebels in north-east India. Still more importantly, they accepted that there was a border problem. Whether by accident, design or bureaucratic rivalry, it was during Vajpayee's visit to Beijing that China attacked Vietnam. New Delhi had developed cordial relations with Hanoi, and the attack forced the Indian delegation to return home. From that point Indian parliamentary opinion imposed a brake on the normalization of Sino-Indian relations.

Kosygin's visit to New Delhi in March 1979 sought above all to turn the Indian government against China. He failed to get the Indian government to call the Chinese attack on Vietnam 'aggression' or to recognize the Heng Samrin government in Kampuchea, which had been installed by the Vietnamese army. He succeeded, however, in signing a long-term cooperation agreement with India. The price paid by Moscow was an increase in the crude oil deliveries. Still more Soviet oil was on offer when Desai made a return visit to Moscow, only three months after Kosygin's talks in New Delhi. Whereas India had previously feared that Moscow was being too friendly with Islamabad, now Desai took the opposite position. He refused to go along with the Kremlin in condemning Pakistan for giving support to opponents of the pro-Soviet revolutionary regime in Kabul.

In July, the Janata government fell and was replaced by the caretaker government of Charan Singh. This had little time for foreign affairs. In the campaign for the national elections of January 1980, Mrs Gandhi and her Congress (I) took a rather more pro-Soviet stance than Janata. In particular, she demanded the recognition of Heng Samrin. Moscow, having burned its fingers in 1977, refrained from endorsing any party other than the CPI and the CPI(M) – which had succeeded in forming an electoral alliance.[19] It is possible that the International Department of the CPSU Central Committee realized that the cost of the CPI backing Indira Gandhi's emergency had been too high in terms of lost votes, and that it should now re-establish itself as a force on the left.

Moscow and Mrs Gandhi again, 1980–4

After Mrs Gandhi's decisive election victory, she at once had to face the problems caused by the Soviet invasion of Afghanistan. She expressed disapproval of the occupation, not only because it represented the entry of Soviet troops into South Asia for the first time, but also because it might encourage the intervention of other powers in the region (see Chapter 3). Although the effect of the American aid to Pakistan was to force India back towards the Soviet Union for its defence needs, Indira Gandhi's attitude to Moscow was cooler and more suspicious after Afghanistan. The Politburo tried to soothe India by sending Gromyko to New Delhi in January 1980, and First Deputy Premier Ivan Arkhipov to discuss economic aid the following month. In July Mrs Gandhi dealt a blow to her relations both with China and with the West by recognizing the Heng Samrin regime in Kampuchea. This was in line with the stance she had taken in opposition. In December 1980 Brezhnev came to Delhi with nearly three hundred people in train, including Gromyko and Arkhipov. This visit, like his previous one in 1973, was built up in the Soviet press, which loudly praised the Soviet-Indian relationship. Brezhnev was welcomed warmly, but the ageing General Secretary and President spent only three hours with Mrs Gandhi. An agreement on trade and on economic and technical cooperation for 1981–5 was signed. India did not shift its position on Afghanistan, and reportedly Mrs Gandhi made it clear, in private, that the presence of Soviet troops was bad for Soviet-Indian relations. Moscow described the meeting as 'frank' and, once again, Afghanistan was not referred to in the communiqué.

The cooling of Soviet-Indian relations is evident from the language used by Brezhnev in the Central Committee report to the 26th Party Congress in February 1981.

> Comrades, a prominent place in the Soviet Union's relations with the newly free countries is, of course, held by our cooperation with India. We welcome the increasing role played by that state in international affairs. Our ties with it are continuing to expand. In both our countries, Soviet-Indian friendship has become a deep-rooted popular tradition.
>
> As a result of the recent negotiations in Delhi with Prime Minister Indira Gandhi and other Indian leaders, the entire range of Soviet-Indian relations has advanced substantially further.
>
> Joint action with peaceful and independent India will continue to be one of the important areas of Soviet foreign policy.

This is not nearly as supportive of Mrs Gandhi as his report to the Congress five years before, but what is significant is that India was the only Third World government (if Afghanistan is excepted) to receive any praise throughout the speech.[20]

India attempted in 1980 and 1981 to improve its relations with Western Europe, the United States, China and Pakistan, and in particular to diversify its sources of arms imports. The Soviet authorities played up the tenth anniversary of the Indo-Soviet friendship treaty in August 1981, whereas India gave it scant attention, and Mrs Gandhi even refused to go to Moscow for a celebration. The advent of the Reagan administration in 1981 – with its policy of confronting the Soviet Union across the globe – was to block the improvement of Indo-American relations. The new policy was to affect India in two ways: by the increase in US naval forces in the Indian Ocean, contrary to India's desire for demilitarization; and by the granting of military aid to Pakistan.

Moscow showed its concern about relations with India in March 1982, with the dispatch of a top-level defence delegation to New Delhi. It was headed by Defence Minister Marshal Dimitry Ustinov and included seventy others – an unprecedented number for a Soviet military delegation to India. No important deal was struck, owing to India's desire to diversify its sources of arms imports. The visit did, however, represent a demonstration of Soviet support for India. A further such demonstration came with the visit of Eduard Shevardnadze (then a candidate member of the Politburo and leader of the Communist Party of Georgia) for the 12th Congress of the CPI at Varanasi, also in March 1982. The CPI confirmed its hostility towards Mrs Gandhi's domestic policies, accusing her of fostering the 'cult of the family' and of allowing corruption at high levels. Shevardnadze expressed appreciation of the 'realistic approach' of the Indian government to the Afghan problem, and successfully urged the party to back Indira Gandhi's foreign policy.[21]

Mrs Gandhi's first visit to Moscow since the invasion of Afghanistan finally took place in September. She again said that Soviet troops should be withdrawn from Afghanistan, but this was omitted from both the Tass report and the joint communiqué. With regard to bilateral relations, the two sides agreed to increase trade by at least 50% by 1986. The Soviet Prime Minister, Nikolai Tikhonov, offered to build a 1,000 MW nuclear power plant, as well as a thermal power plant almost as large, and to expand the Visakhapatnam steel plant. Mrs Gandhi complained about the opposition she was getting from the CPI to her domestic policies. An article by Rostislav Ulianovsky, a deputy head of the Central Committee International Department with responsibility for South Asia, which appeared in the Soviet journal *Asia and Africa Today*, may have been a response to this. It expressed only qualified support for her stand against domestic reaction. On the question of China, both Moscow and New Delhi were now actively seeking better relations with Beijing. Brezhnev's Tashkent speech in March 1982 calling for confidence-building measures on the border was paralleled by the Indian Defence Ministry's removal of China from the category of a principal threat.[22]

The death of Brezhnev caused Mrs Gandhi to visit Moscow again – for the funeral in November 1982. She met Iury Andropov, the new General Secretary, who at that time did not seem to give India the priority it had received under Brezhnev. Observers noted the time given to Pakistan's President, General Zia ul-Haq, at the funeral, while the Afghan leader, Babrak Karmal, was all but ignored. It seemed that Moscow was stepping up a dialogue with Pakistan in order to achieve a settlement in Afghanistan. This appeared to be in accordance with the Indian desire for a Soviet withdrawal. In his first regular Central Committee Plenum speech, Andropov followed Brezhnev at the 26th Congress in singling out Soviet-Indian relations for a positive mention.[23] Indira Gandhi announced in March 1983 that Andropov had accepted an invitation to visit New Delhi. This would have been his first trip outside the Soviet bloc since becoming General Secretary, and again probably reflected the priority he had come to give to India, especially perhaps at a time of improving Sino-Soviet relations.[24] The visit never materialized, however, owing to Andropov's poor health.

Meanwhile in June 1983, Mrs Gandhi sent a letter to Andropov (via Yogendra Sharma, a CPI member critical of the party's anti-Indira Gandhi decision of 1978), complaining that the CPI was joining 'unholy rightist forces' which were intent on removing her from power. She asked the Soviet Central Committee to tell the CPI to give her support. According to the Indian journalist Kuldip Nayar, the Andropov leadership was more willing than the Brezhnev leadership to tell the CPI to back her domestic policy. But the CPI annual conference in September 1983 attacked the 'communal politics' of Indira Gandhi. Andropov does not seem to have replied to Mrs Gandhi's request.[25] In July, however, the Kremlin showed its regard for her by inviting her son and prospective successor, Rajiv Gandhi (Sanjay having been killed in an air crash), to Moscow. There he met various leaders, including Ustinov, Gromyko and Arkhipov, as well as Boris Ponomaryov, a Politburo candidate member and head of the International Department.

During Andropov's period in office as General Secretary, both the USSR and India were pursuing better relations with Pakistan, China and America. Moscow stepped up its carrot-and-stick policy with regard to Islamabad, by increasing economic aid but at the same time threatening to carry the Afghan war into the resistance bases in Pakistan. In the middle of 1983, agreement over Afghanistan between the two governments was close but then evaporated, either because of military opposition to Andropov, or more probably because the United States pressured the Zia regime into a tougher line. Since Andropov was unable to attend Politburo meetings, let alone travel, the Politburo agreed that Ustinov, at that time a very influential member of the leadership, should go to India in his stead. The visit was, however, postponed owing to Andropov's imminent death, which occurred in February 1984. Mrs Gandhi and Zia both travelled to Moscow for the funeral. The new General Secretary, Konstantin Chernenko, spoke with Indira Gandhi for twenty-five minutes, but his refusal of Zia's request for a meeting indicated a harder Soviet line on Afghanistan.

Ustinov's visit went ahead in March. The Indian media played up the occasion (in contrast to their reaction to his visit of 1982). The Defence Minister was given the treatment normally received by a head of state; he even stayed at the Rashtrapati Bhavan (Presidential Palace). His 55-member delegation included Marshal Sergei Akhromeev (the First Deputy Chief of the General Staff) and a strong naval contingent including Admiral Sergei Gorshkov. They agreed to supply India with weapons of the same sophistication as they sold to members of the Warsaw Pact. Ustinov promised that the USSR would keep India supplied with oil if the Gulf war should interrupt deliveries from the Middle East. The message received in Delhi was that Moscow wished to expand its relations with India. During Mrs Gandhi's discussions with Ustinov, which once again took place solely in the presence of a Soviet interpreter, both sides expressed concern about the militarization of Pakistan. There was talk of an Indo-Soviet strategic consensus. Both Moscow and New Delhi blamed Pakistan for encouraging Sikh terrorism. Ustinov said that Chernenko would visit India, but, as in the case of Andropov, his health was to prevent this.

While the Soviet Union was putting more emphasis on its friendship with India, however, India was continuing to diversify its foreign relations. In May US Vice-President George Bush visited both India and Pakistan. It was being widely predicted in the early 1980s that India would be forced to turn more and more to the West for the technology it needed for its economy, as the Soviet Union would be increasingly unable to supply the level required. In 1984 the US navy visited Indian ports for the first time for thirteen years, and the Indian Chief of Staff, General A.S. Vaidya, visited Washington to discuss arms purchases. There was evidence of a desire within the Reagan administration to redress the balance of the South Asian policy of the United States and to restore better relations with India.[26]

New generations: Moscow and Rajiv Gandhi, 1984–7

Rajiv Gandhi became Prime Minister on 31 October 1984, only hours after the assassination of his mother by two Sikhs among her bodyguard. In the elections held at the end of December, the Congress (I) won its largest ever number of seats and votes – 401 out of 508 seats in the Lok Sabha, with nearly 50% of the vote. In the United States, hopes were raised that the 40-year-old leader, with his Italian wife and his interest in technology, would move India to a more pro-Western form of non-alignment. He was, in Stephen P. Cohen's words, 'not tied down by prejudices of the past'.[27] The US Secretary of State, George Shultz, met Rajiv at his mother's funeral, and a number of American politicians who visited the young Prime Minister in succeeding months 'returned convinced that the time was ripe for achieving a breakthrough in Indo-US relations'. Shultz told Rajiv that the United States would try to treat India more favourably, without reducing the American commitment to Pakistan. The military aid to Pakistan, according to Shultz, made Pakistan less likely to see a need for nuclear weapons.[28]

There is little doubt that Moscow was worried by these developments. Chernenko's sympathy message to Rajiv emphasized Indira Gandhi's concern for Indo-Soviet ties. Tikhonov travelled to New Delhi for the funeral, and Rajiv assured him that he would continue the policies of his mother and grandfather. From the time of the assassination, Soviet propaganda sought to fan anti-American feeling by accusing the CIA and Pakistan of being behind the Sikh terrorists. The assassination, according to *Pravda*, was a plot to destabilize India.[29] The journal *International Affairs* for April 1985 quoted an Indian government White Paper on the foreign backers of the Khalistanis (the supporters of an independent Sikh state of Khalistan) and an *India Today* article linking them with Senator Jesse Helms and US intelligence agencies. The Soviet media gave an unqualified welcome to Rajiv's electoral victory, which they saw as a defeat for communalism. He was described as an 'outstanding statesman'. The Soviet Union also approved the summit conference of six nations, held in New Delhi in January 1985 and chaired by Rajiv, which appealed for a halt to the arms race (see Chapter 4).[30]

The appointment of Mikhail Gorbachev as General Secretary in March 1985 meant that the USSR now also had a (relatively) young leader, with a new style and, like Rajiv, a pronounced commitment to technological progress. As early as July, the replacement of Gromyko as Foreign Minister by Shevardnadze, who was known as a reformer in Georgia, indicated Gorbachev's determination to put his own stamp on foreign policy. His concern with domestic economic growth raised the possibility that he might try to reduce the cost of foreign involvement, including the commitment to India. But Gorbachev showed the importance he attached to India by meeting Rajiv no less than three times in 1985 – at Chernenko's funeral in March, and at bilateral summits in Moscow in May and October. No other Third World leader received similar attention.[31]

The discovery of a French- and Soviet-linked spy-ring in New Delhi in April caused some embarrassment in the Indian capital, but no lasting damage. Rajiv's visit to Moscow in May was his first official visit abroad since becoming Prime Minister, excluding Chernenko's funeral and a visit to Bhutan. Reversing the priority of his mother in 1981–2, he visited Washington only in June, after Moscow. The joint communiqué after the Moscow visit of 21–26 May showed no movement on the Indian side towards the Soviet positions on Afghanistan, on which the Indians found the Soviet negotiators to be less rigid, or on the collective security system in Asia. Both questions were ignored in the communiqué. For the first time since the Sino-Soviet split, the Soviet team at an Indo-Soviet summit referred to China in friendly terms, and expressed optimism that relations would improve. According to Gujral, the Soviet leaders wanted Rajiv to act as a mediator between the two superpowers, at a time when direct meetings between the leaders were not taking place. In line with the practice of Brezhnev and Mrs Gandhi, the two new leaders signed a 15-year cooperation agreement. Moscow opened a one billion rouble credit line.[32]

Rajiv's visit to the United States was successful; the Americans reduced the limits on technological exports, and the Indians agreed to improve conditions for American business. In fact, however, overall US-Indian trade fell in 1985, with the increase in Indian imports from the United States being smaller than the decline in Indian exports to America.[33] Iqbal Narain of the Indian Council for Social Science Research commented at the beginning of 1986: 'while basically remaining non-aligned and depending largely on the time-tested Soviet support for building up and strengthening India's defense structure, Rajiv is tending to open up and widen his options, much more than his grandfather and mother did, in terms of closer ties with Europe, Japan and even the US'.[34]

Soviet concern to maintain ties with India was evident in a comment made in October 1985 by Mikhail Kapitsa, at that time Deputy Foreign Minister and now Director of the IOS. He assured a

Pakistan newspaper that his country wished to be friendly with all the South Asian states, but 'in the case of a problem between India and its neighbours, we will side with India'.[35] Rajiv's October visit to Gorbachev in Moscow was an unexpected stopover on the way back from his address to the UN General Assembly and a meeting with Reagan. He denied speculation that he was acting as the mediator between the superpowers. Tass reported that the participants in the Indo-Soviet summit noted the 'high level of development of bilateral relations on the stable basis of the [1971] treaty'. It added that disarmament and other international affairs, presumably Afghanistan, were also discussed.[36] Two days later *Pravda* published an article by President Gromyko commemorating Indira Gandhi, on the anniversary of her death, and emphasizing her friendship for the Soviet Union. Gromyko expressed satisfaction that Rajiv's government 'demonstrates continuity with the line of Indira Gandhi'.[37] Western commentators were inclined to see such Soviet statements as reflecting anxiety. Less than a month later, however, according to the Press Trust of India, trade officials from the two countries signed an agreement intended to double (*sic*) bilateral trade in 1986.[38]

The flow of visits and agreements since then does suggest, indeed, that both sides see advantage in increasing their links. On 23 December 1985 the trade ministers of the two countries signed an agreement seeking to double the value of their trade in the period 1986–90 over 1981–5.[39] In the Central Committee report to the 27th Party Congress, February-March 1986, Gorbachev avoided discussion of the domestic or foreign policy of any Third World country, but mentioned the Soviet-Indian summit before his meetings with French President François Mitterrand and President Reagan.[40] In April Arkhipov attended the 10th meeting of the Joint Economic Commission in New Delhi, which discussed cooperation in electronics and computer manufacture as well as in more traditional areas.[41] In June the Indian Foreign Minister, P. Shiv Shankar, visited Gorbachev and Shevardnadze in Moscow. The Tass communiqué reported that the participants had condemned terrorism and the encouragement of terrorism from outside – an implicit attack on Pakistan and possibly the United States for allegedly supporting pro-Khalistan terrorist activities.[42] A *Pravda* article on 22 July was more explicit in attacking both the Zia regime and the plan of the Reagan administration to give it aid worth $4 billion over the period 1988–93. It accused Washington of conniving at Pakistan's desire for nuclear weapons, and accused the CIA in particular of helping Pakistan to interfere in the affairs of Afghanistan and India. The article cited *Times of India* and *Hindustan Times* reports about Pakistan training Sikh terrorists.[43]

Gorbachev's visit to New Delhi, November 1986

Engine trouble in his aeroplane forced Rajiv to make another (unexpected) visit to Moscow in August. Back in New Delhi, he announced that Gorbachev was likely to visit the Indian capital later in the year. The 'official friendly visit' of 25–28 November was the culmination of a series of exchanges between trade, defence and foreign ministers and officials of the two countries. Both sides were anxious that the visit should be an unmistakable success. The Soviet press gave it extensive front-page treatment, as was to be expected. What was more significant was the willingness of the Indian government to play up the visit. The state-controlled television station ran a series of programmes on the USSR and Indo-Soviet relations. On 23 November the Indian edition of Gorbachev's speeches was published in Delhi (in English). Both Foreign Minister Narayan Dutt Tiwari and President Zail Singh spoke at the launch at the Rashtrapati Bhavan.[44] The Indian government signalled to the independent press to build up the visit. Posters of Rajiv and Gorbachev, and of the two of them with their wives, appeared all over Delhi. Gorbachev was accompanied by Shevardnadze, Dobrynin, the Central Committee Secretary and head of the International Department, Deputy Prime Minister Vladimir Kamentsev, Akhromeev – Defence Minister Marshal Sergei Sokolov was believed to be unwell – and Vorontsov, the First Deputy Foreign Minister. The discussions included nearly ten hours of private talks between the two leaders, in which Rajiv followed his mother's custom and was accompanied by no other Indian, relying on the Soviet interpreter.

The importance of the cultural agreement should not be overlooked. Details were filled out regarding the holding of festivals in each other's country, which had been agreed in March 1986. The Festival of India in the USSR, to commemorate the fortieth anniversary of India's independence, would begin in July 1987, and the Festival of the USSR in India, devoted to the seventieth anniversary of the Bolshevik Revolution, would begin in November 1987.[45]

The two sides signed an agreement on economic and technical cooperation which, according to both leaders, was the 'largest in the history' of Soviet-Indian relations.[46] The Soviet Union extended a soft credit of 1.5 billion roubles (most of which was at $2\frac{1}{2}\%$ interest and repayable over 17 years), on top of the billion roubles extended the previous year. Rajiv announced that the two countries were to increase their trade by about two-and-a-half times by 1992. New areas of trade would be explored, and to this end a delegation from the Academy of Sciences of the USSR, headed by Gury Marchuk, the Academy's President, would be coming to India. It was agreed that, for the first time, joint ventures between Soviet enterprises and Indian companies in the private sector would be established.[47] This was in line with the overall policies of the two new leaders, both of whom were committed to decentralizing economic decision-making.

As far as defence matters were concerned, the first batch of MiG-29s was about to be delivered to India, before any of the Warsaw Treaty Organization countries had received them. The Indians had been pleased when US Defense Secretary Caspar Weinberger seemed willing in October, on the first ever visit of an American Defense Secretary to New Delhi, to allow the transfer of the Cray super-computer and other civilian and military technologies to India. To the dismay of the Indians, however, Weinberger then went on to Islamabad and offered the AWACS (airborne warning and control system) to Pakistan. During the Gorbachev visit, the Soviet arms specialists offered anti-AWACS equipment to the Indians, but the latter preferred to leave the offer on the shelf for the time being.[48]

Although Afghanistan did not figure in the communiqué,[49] the two sides appeared to be closer together on the issue than in the past. Gorbachev seemed sincere in his desire for a Soviet withdrawal. Indo-Pakistani relations had deteriorated to the point at which Rajiv had even accused Pakistan, in October, of being involved in an attempt on his life.[50] A serious worry for India was the improving state of Sino-Soviet relations. In his important speech on security in the Asia-Pacific region at Vladivostok on 28 July 1986, Gorbachev had attacked the United States and Japan, but had spoken positively of China. He had proposed a Helsinki-style conference for the Asia-Pacific region, in the framework of creating a 'comprehensive system of international security'. Even though he had taken care to praise 'the great India' as the 'recognized leader' of the NAM, and to commend the state of Soviet-Indian relations, Indians could not help wondering whether the normalization of Sino-Soviet relations would be at India's expense.[51] In September Nikolai Talyzin, candidate member of the Politburo, First Deputy Prime Minister and head of Gosplan USSR, had visited China – the first person of Politburo level to do so since 1969. There was tension on India's borders with both Pakistan and China, and India had expressed concern also about nuclear cooperation between its two adversaries.

It was significant that, at the banquet on 25 November, Rajiv effusively praised the 1971 treaty, in a way not seen since the invasion of Afghanistan. 'It remains a source of strength for our respective countries. Its importance has increased in the context of the current world situation and recent events in our part of the world.'[52] This reference 'elated' the visitors. It was also a signal of India's willingness to draw on Soviet help, should it be threatened in any regional conflicts.[53] During Gorbachev's visit, Indian journalists (and presumably Indian politicians) pressed him to say that in the event of a military conflict between India and either Pakistan or China, the Soviet Union would support India. Although he stated that 'what we do to improve relations with China will not weaken our relations with India,'[54] essentially reiterating his earlier assertion that 'we shall not make a single step that could damage India's real interests', he did not make any commitment.[55] According to *The Statesman*, however, he had privately assured Rajiv of Soviet support in such a situation.[56] Gorbachev emphasized his desire for disagreements in the region to be resolved peacefully.[57] The communiqué did not mention Gorbachev's 'Asian Helsinki' proposals, and different formulations were used for the two sides' views on international security. Ironically, whereas previously India had rejected Brezhnev's proposal for a collective security system in Asia because, among other things, it was clearly aimed against China, it was now unhappy about Gorbachev's proposal precisely because it did include China.[58]

From the Soviet view, perhaps the most important gain of the visit was the 'Delhi declaration on the principles of a nuclear-weapon-free and non-violent world'.[59] The Reagan administration's decision to 'break out' of the SALT II limits, which was announced during the visit, increased the credibility of the Soviet position. On most other foreign-policy issues – the Indian Ocean and Diego Garcia, the Middle East, South-East Asia, southern Africa and Nicaragua – the positions of the two sides were very close, and therefore were critical of those of the United States.[60] The Soviet media for months afterwards found it helpful to make laudatory references to Indian foreign policy in general and the Delhi declaration in particular. *India Today* referred (with some hyperbole) to the results of the visit as a 'geo-political bombshell'. 'Overnight, a superpower and the leader of the increasingly influential Non-Aligned Movement (NAM) transformed what has been a somewhat hesitant and diffident relationship into an aggressive new partnership that could have far-reaching consequences for international diplomacy.'[61]

The visit was seen as a personal triumph for Rajiv, and the enthusiasm of both Congress (I) and opposition MPs for Gorbachev during his speech to the Indian parliament seemed a ringing endorsement of Rajiv's foreign policy.[62] Gorbachev held meetings with the leaders of the CPI (seventy-five minutes) and CPI(M) (forty-five minutes). It was the first time since the split in 1964 that CPI(M) leaders had met the Soviet General Secretary. The Tass communiqués concerning the meetings avoided mention of Indian internal matters, beyond reporting the view of the General Secretary of the CPI(M), E.M.S. Namboodiripad, that the struggle of Indian workers for their rights coincided with the struggle against the nuclear threat. It is a matter for speculation whether Gorbachev was trying to persuade the two parties to back Rajiv's domestic policy as well as his foreign policy.[63] Subsequent Soviet propaganda praised Rajiv even more than before the visit. Perhaps the main purpose of the Gorbachev show from the Indian viewpoint, however, was to put pressure on the Americans. Essentially, India wanted the United States to supply it with technology, but not to give the latest weapons to Pakistan. After Weinberger's offer to Zia, Rajiv may have wanted to signal to Washington that India could not be taken for granted.

Throughout 1987 Rajiv continued to seek maximum advantages from both Washington and Moscow. The Soviet Union avoided giving any open backing to India during the border clashes which occurred in the early part of the year with both Pakistan and China (the former was defused in February after Zia travelled to watch the Test Match at Jaipur with Rajiv). When the Prime Minister arrived in Moscow in July to open the Festival of India, he was received extremely warmly, and a twelve-year agreement on scientific cooperation was signed. In October, during a visit to Washington, he persuaded the Americans to allow India to import a number of defence systems, and obtained American agreement to train Indian administrators. Although CPI General Secretary Rajeshwara Rao denounced the government for expanding ties with the United States, Soviet diplomats denied any concern at these developments. Nevertheless, Moscow seemed to be bending over backwards to find ways of increasing links with India. In November Soviet Prime Minister Nikolai Ryzhkov visited India to open the Festival of the USSR. The two sides agreed to increase trade by 25% in 1988, and the Soviet Union agreed to supply 6.5 million tonnes of petroleum products in the course of 1988, on terms described as 'very favourable'.[64] The Soviet decision to start withdrawing its troops from Afghanistan in May 1988 met India's long-expressed wishes. It did not, however, lead to any immediate improvement in the international relations of the region that might serve to reduce ties between Moscow and New Delhi.

3

THE ASIAN CONTEXT

This chapter explores the core of the relationship between the Soviet Union and India: namely, the regional context in which the relationship is located, and which provides the main reason for its lasting success.

It is somewhat artificial to divide the 'Asian' from the 'global' aspects of the Soviet-Indian relationship, since global factors such as Soviet-American competition are present in the regional tensions among the Asian powers. The term 'Asian' is here used to refer to the countries close to India (i.e., it covers a region wider than what is conventionally known as South Asia, since it includes China). Matters concerning the Indian Ocean are considered in the context of global issues, since these may relate to countries as far away as South Africa. Similarly, Indo-American relations are considered in the chapter on the global context of the relationship, except where they relate purely to the region.

There is a lack of symmetry in the importance attached by the Soviet and Indian sides to the regional and the global aspects of the relationship. Whereas India's main concern in the relationship is regional security, for the Soviet Union both regional security and the support of India for Soviet positions in global forums have been of central significance. For Moscow, South Asia is one of the regions in which the global competition between the two superpowers, and (at times) between the Soviet Union and China, takes place. It is of much less significance than Europe or East Asia, but its proximity to China and Afghanistan nevertheless lends it importance. On the other hand, for New Delhi the support which the USSR has given in the past in India's conflicts with its neighbours, and its potential for giving support in the region in the future, form the key rationale for the Soviet-Indian relationship. This factor is of greater importance than the economic assistance provided by the Soviet Union to India, at least some of which could have been found elsewhere, if not on such favourable terms.

The alignments at present found in South Asia bear a considerable resemblance to those which would have been expected by the Indian strategist of the fourth century BC, Kautilya. His strategic thinking was based on the axiom that two countries which bordered on one another would be enemies. But since, according to Kautilya, 'my enemy's enemy is my friend', it followed that two countries which bordered another country, but lacked a common frontier, should have good relations. On this basis, India would be hostile to Pakistan and China, and friendly to Afghanistan and the Soviet Union (in circumstances in which these were the enemies of Pakistan and China respectively).

It should be noted here that the northwestern part of Kashmir, which borders on Afghanistan, is controlled by Pakistan. India formally claims this zone, and Soviet maps depict it as part of India. Without the Pakistani presence, India would not only border on Afghanistan but come within 100 miles of the Soviet republic of Tajikistan. Pakistan's control of the area gives it a land bridge to China, on which the Karakoram highway was completed in 1978. The importance of this strategic link for both China and Pakistan gives them a common interest in preventing India from gaining control over the territory. Conversely, the proximity of the highway to the Wakhan Corridor in Afghanistan, and to the Soviet Union itself, is likely to be of considerable concern to Moscow, as well as having symbolic significance in its location at what was the meeting-point of the Russian, Chinese, British and Persian empires in the nineteenth century.

Indian policy in the region

The Indian scholar J.P. Premdev suggests that Nehru, in formulating India's foreign policy, accepted Kautilya's views and pursued friendship with the Soviet Union and Afghanistan.[1] Nehru himself rather unsuccessfully also sought good relations with China; and in the 1970s, after the Bangladesh war, both Mrs Gandhi and Janata tried to improve relations with China and Pakistan. After 1979, however, relations with China were variable, while those with Pakistan were generally poor. Indeed India has problems in its relations with most of its neighbours: with Bangladesh over the Farakka Barrage, and over intrusions of Bengalis from Bangladesh; with Sri Lanka over the position of the Tamil minority there; and (over water resources and migration) with Nepal, which has oscillated between emphasizing its relations with India and giving priority to those with China. India's relations with Burma have been quite good. It is not difficult to understand the anxieties felt by India's weaker neighbours. Its assistance to East Bengal in 1971 speeded up the disintegration of Pakistan. Its annexation of Sikkim in 1975 and the dispatch of Indian troops to Sri Lanka, albeit with the agreement of the latter's president in 1987, are clear signs of India's willingness, on occasion, to project military force into neighbouring countries. The Indian view that the countries in the region should be democracies is an irritant to their military and one-party dictatorships.

The events of 1971 left India the dominant power in South Asia. Agha Shahi, who was Pakistan's Minister of External Affairs until 1982, has spoken of 'India's determination ... to assert a right to hegemony over the smaller nations of South Asia'.[2] Less histrionically, the historian Surjit Mansingh refers to Indira Gandhi's desire for India to be able to influence its neighbours without asserting its power.[3] A key to this was the exclusion of the superpowers and China from the ability to influence South Asian affairs. Another was the development of India's own military potential, begun in response to its humiliation following the Chinese invasion of 1962. It was while Mrs Gandhi was in office that the Indian armed forces swelled to the size of a major international force, with an army approaching one million men.[4] By 1987 India had 1,262,000 people serving in the armed forces, the third largest in the world after the USSR and China.[5] Nevertheless, in comparison with other Third World countries, it maintained a low defence budget, no more than 3–4% per annum in the period 1964–84,[6] and its reluctance to develop nuclear weapons, after showing the capacity to do so in 1974, was another sign of restraint. Between 1981, the year in which the United States systematically stepped up its military aid programme to Pakistan, and 1986, Indian defence spending rose 5.6%

per annum.[7] In March 1987, for reasons not made clear but presumably related to the deteriorating regional situation as well as to the programme for equipment modernization, the defence budget for 1987–8 was raised by 43% over the original estimates for the preceding year.[8]

In the diplomatic sphere, too, India has played a leading role. In December 1985, under Rajiv Gandhi, the South Asia Association for Regional Cooperation (SAARC) was established, with seven members – India, Pakistan, Bangladesh, Sri Lanka, Nepal, Bhutan and the Maldives. The SAARC Charter explicitly debarred 'bilateral and contentious issues' from being discussed, but SAARC was not seen solely as an economic body. Rather, it had an implicit security dimension, and since it excluded the superpowers and China it may be said to have assisted India's hegemony in the region.

Soviet policy

The Soviet Union's principal concern in South Asia has been to prevent the region, or any part of it, from falling under the dominance of the USA or China. In its willingness to settle for non-alignment rather than insisting on membership of military blocs or seeking military bases, it has shown sensitivity to national feelings and has gained an advantage over the USA.[9] It was the China factor which was of major importance in the Soviet need for friendship with India.[10] Emphasizing the regional (as opposed to the economic or NAM) aspects of Soviet interests in India, Stephen P. Cohen wrote in an article in 1985: 'Soviet interest in South Asia is primarily strategic in nature, deriving almost entirely from the long-standing Sino-Soviet conflict.' He supported this by reference to the way the Soviet-Indian relationship has varied according to Chinese links with Moscow and New Delhi. 'Nothing brings Soviet generals to New Delhi bearing gifts of military hardware faster than the prospect of Sino-Indian negotiations over their border dispute.'[11] Although this latter statement held for the 1970s and early 1980s, it would be invalid for the current period of 'new political thinking', when Sino-Soviet relations are improving. Cohen suggests that it is not so much China on its own that was seen as a threat, but China in alliance with Pakistan and the USA.[12] By the mid-1980s the US link with Pakistan was surely evoking greater concern in Moscow than the Sino-Pakistani connection.

In order to deny the United States and China influence in South Asia, the Soviet Union needs to create a situation in which no country in the region feels compelled to call on outside help to deal with its neighbours. Whereas India seeks to avoid superpower interference in the region, Pakistan has felt compelled to seek the assistance of outside powers to make up for the disparity between its own strength and that of India. In the 1960s and 1970s 'ties with Beijing . . . remained the cornerstone of Islamabad's policy'. China offered $620 million in assistance to Pakistan between 1964 and 1979, which compensated for Pakistan's losses in the 1971 war and supplied most of its tanks and aircraft.[13] If outside help is to be obviated, Pakistan needs to be assured that India will not use its superior military strength against it. The logic of this position is that there will be a tendency for Moscow to seek to reconcile the interests of India and Pakistan and to encourage cooperation between them. Kosygin achieved this at Tashkent in 1966, and the relationship remained comparatively stable up to the start of hostilities in 1971. It is true that other factors, such as relations with China and the United States, and the consequences of the invasion of Afghanistan, have often led Moscow to attack Islamabad publicly and with venom, but this does not detract from its basic interest in South Asian stability. Soviet attempts to calm the Indo-Pakistani relationship come into conflict, however, with the Indian desire to stop the superpowers interfering in the region.[14] But then, again, this objective is subordinate to India's primary aim of ensuring strategic superiority over its neighbours, and seeking whatever outside help is needed for the purpose.

The invasion of Afghanistan

The Janata government elected in 1977 did not abrogate the Indo-Soviet friendship treaty and, contrary to the pre-election statements of its leaders, maintained relations with the Soviet Union on much the same level as before. Foreign Minister Vajpayee said that the 'responsibilities of power' had changed his perspective.[15] This suggests that the relationship corresponded to the geopolitical 'Kautilyan' interests of India. The invasion of Afghanistan, however, threatened to put the relationship under strain. When, at the end of December 1979, the Soviet Union informed India that it had sent forces into Afghanistan (without prior notification to New

Delhi), there was less than a week to go before the Indian general election. The caretaker government of Charan Singh informed the Soviet ambassador of 'India's deep concern', and spoke of 'far-reaching and adverse consequences' for the whole of South Asia. It demanded the withdrawal of Soviet troops.[16] Indira Gandhi put the Soviet invasion in the context of other foreign involvement. She said on 2 January 1980: 'I am strongly against any interference. But in Afghanistan the Soviet interference is not one-sided. Other interferences are going on there.'[17] After returning to office, she made clear her opposition to the Soviet action, and for the remainder of her term in power it seemed that the invasion had made her more wary of Moscow than before. The other non-communist parties were more forthright in their criticisms than she was, and one may speculate as to whether they would have tilted away from the Soviet Union if they had won the election. It is quite possible that the changes in India's strategic environment following the Soviet occupation of Afghanistan might have forced another Desai government back towards the Soviet Union.

Indira Gandhi resumed the office of prime minister on 14 January 1980. Even before this she had advised officials in the Foreign Office to avoid being drawn into the chorus of condemnation of the Soviet Union over Afghanistan. The Indian envoy at the UN General Assembly, Brajesh Mishra, took this still further in the debate of 11 January. He accepted the Soviet claim that Afghanistan had invited the Soviet troops. He added that India hoped they would not remain 'a day longer than necessary', implying that India saw the need for their presence.[18] According to Nihal Singh, it was widely believed that this speech had been drafted by T.N. Kaul.[19] India abstained on the General Assembly motion calling for the withdrawal of 'foreign' troops, which was passed by 104 votes to 18, with the support of most non-aligned countries. There were 18 abstentions. India's stance called into question its commitment to the NAM, since the principles of non-alignment were directly opposed to superpower intervention in the affairs of small states. V.P. Dutt has suggested that the initial Indian stance at the United Nations was the result of confusion caused by the change of government in New Delhi, although Partha Ghosh and Rajaran Panda claim that Mishra was acting under Mrs Gandhi's instructions.[20] Certainly, soon after coming to office, she made clear India's opposition: 'No country is justified in entering another country.'[21] Foreign Minister P.V.

Narasimha Rao spelt it out further to the Lok Sabha on 23 January. 'As the Prime Minister has clearly indicated, we are against the presence of foreign troops and bases in any country. We have expressed our hope that Soviet forces will withdraw from Afghanistan.'[22]

Moscow was probably grateful that Mrs Gandhi's government followed the Soviet view in insisting on seeing the Soviet action in the context of the help given by Pakistan, the United States and China to the Afghan resistance in the preceding period. But the Soviet leaders were presumably concerned that India should fully understand their position, and accept it as much as possible. Theoretically, it is possible that it was not in Moscow's interests for India to appear to be too close to the Soviet position on Afghanistan, since this might have undermined its credibility in the NAM and at the UN, as well as its ability to defend Soviet policies where these coincided with Soviet interests. It is unlikely that the Kremlin perceived things in this way. The Soviet Union was so isolated by international reaction to its invasion of Afghanistan that it would have welcomed public support from India. The Politburo sent Gromyko to New Delhi in mid-February to try to win India round. It is probably an indication of Mrs Gandhi's reaction to the invasion that the British Foreign Secretary, Lord Carrington, Carter's envoy, Clark Clifford, and President Giscard d'Estaing had all been received in New Delhi and had discussed Afghanistan with representatives of the Indian government before the talks with Gromyko.

The widespread hostility in India to the Soviet invasion was due not only to the attack it represented on the self-determination of an independent state, but also to the fact that it brought Soviet forces nearer to India. In the past, Afghanistan had been closely linked to India, and it was regarded by many Indians as part of South Asia. The Soviet presence, therefore, was a potential threat to India's hegemony in the region. More important, it raised the danger of a countervailing presence of the United States in Pakistan, or at least of the United States arming Pakistan so as to enable it to resist Soviet expansion and assist the Afghan rebels. According to the Indian perception, arms transferred to Pakistan in the past on the pretext of helping it to resist communism had been used against India. In Bimal Prasad's words, 'recent history has clearly shown that often when Pakistan was excessively armed, on whatever pretext, India had to bear the brunt and face a war with that country.'[23] The Carter administration offered the Zia regime $400 million worth of military assistance. Pakistan's dismissal of the offer as 'peanuts' left open the possibility of a higher offer in future.

We have no reliable account of the discussions of February 1980 between Gromyko and Indira Gandhi. It seems that his attempts to gain India's support for the invasion 'totally failed'.[24] On the other hand, Narashimha Rao denounced the United States for causing the situation in South Asia to escalate. According to the Indian side, Gromyko resisted pressure for a withdrawal date,[25] and expressed willingness to pull out only under the 'proper conditions'. The joint communiqué omitted any mention of Afghanistan – an indication of the lack of agreement between the two sides.[26] However, the Soviet government remained eager to appease New Delhi, and in May an Indian Defence Ministry delegation visited Moscow. It was granted $1.6 billion credit on easy terms, involving MiG-25 reconnaissance-interceptor aircraft and T-72 tanks. Mrs Gandhi's desire for continued good relations with Moscow was not in doubt. But her government felt threatened by the consequences of the Soviet invasion, and sought to mediate between Moscow, Kabul, Islamabad and Washington. After a visit to Moscow in this connection, Narasimha Rao told the Lok Sabha on 17 June that there was not much hope of a speedy Soviet withdrawal. He continued: 'It is time for us to ask ourselves the question whether the Soviet troops meant for assisting in Afghanistan have not become, or are not likely to become, a pretext of those who wish to create further instability in that country.'[27]

The Pakistan factor

Indian fears that the invasion of Afghanistan would lead to the rearming of Pakistan proved justified. The American military aid did indeed allow Pakistan to assist the Afghan resistance and to develop its own military forces and economy. The USA's designation of Pakistan as a front-line state, a bulwark against Soviet expansionism, was to cause tremendous concern in India, because of its fears that Pakistani weapons would be used against it. In March 1981 Washington offered Islamabad $2.5 billion in military and economic aid, and in September Islamabad accepted a package worth $3.2 billion over six years. In addition, Saudi Arabia paid for deliveries of F-16 jet aircraft. The threat of growing military ties between the United States and Pakistan led Mrs Gandhi, despite her wish to distance herself from Soviet policy, to receive personally both Ogarkov and Gorshkov when they visited India in spring and autumn 1981 respectively. By January 1982, Mrs Gandhi was saying: 'I think the Soviet Union would like to get out of Afghanistan ... but I do not think the others want them to.' Pakistan was gaining American aid, and the Americans were enjoying the Soviet Union's difficulties. The West, Mrs Gandhi maintained in February, had contributed to the crisis by creating Soviet fears of encirclement.[28]

It would be wrong to assume from the above that the US-Pakistan relationship was smooth. In US eyes, to quote William Griffith's apt description, Pakistan was a 'partial, recent, reluctant and suspicious ally of the United States'.[29] In the Pakistani perception, the United States had let Pakistan down in 1962, 1971 and again in the 1980s over the nuclear programme. Having received the 1981 aid package, Pakistan did not sign any treaty of alliance, but remained a member of the NAM. Nor did it become directly involved in the war against the Kabul regime, apart from some incidents on the border.[30]

It has been widely reported, however, that in return for American assistance, Pakistan has cooperated with US military plans in a number of ways. Since 1983 the American P-3 surveillance aircraft, used to monitor Soviet ships and nuclear submarines, has allegedly used Pakistani airfields. In 1985, the US Defense Secretary, Caspar Weinberger, reported to Congress on the need for sites for arms stores, naval bases and airfields in South-West Asia. The American aim has been to draw Pakistan into support for the United States Central Command (CENTCOM). This has been operating since 1983 as the successor to the Rapid Deployment Force created by President Carter, and covers the Indian Ocean and 44 littoral states, including the Persian Gulf region, Afghanistan and Pakistan. American planners have called for the establishment of base facilities in Pakistan to assist the dispatch of forces to the Gulf. Further, Pakistan has refused an Indian proposal to include in an Indo-Pakistani peace treaty a clause involving a denial of military bases to foreign powers.[31] Soviet commentators, not unnaturally, have claimed that the motive behind the USA's assistance to Pakistan is, not to counter 'an outside threat', but to use Pakistani territory and forces in CENTCOM interventions in South-West Asia and the

Middle East, and moreover to pose a threat to India.[32] In May 1987, for example, the Soviet Foreign Ministry declared that Pakistan's participation in American plans threatened the security of India, Afghanistan, the Soviet Union and other countries.[33] At the same time the Indian Minister of External Affairs, N.D. Tiwari, cancelled his planned visit to Washington because India believed that the United States was about to approve the leasing of AWACS to Pakistan.[34]

The aid programme agreed in 1982 meant that the US replaced China as Pakistan's main arms supplier. Pakistan thus became the third largest recipient of US aid (after Israel and Egypt)[35] – an indication of its importance to the United States. In March 1986 Washington and Islamabad agreed a new aid package for 1987–93, totalling \$4.02 billion, on favourable terms.[36] The United States has been unwilling to meet all Pakistani requests for state-of-the-art military equipment, but the possibility of sales of Gruman airborne early-warning E-2C Hawkeyes or of AWACS evoked concern in India. Despite Pakistan's claim that the aircraft are needed to monitor incursions from the Afghan border, India considers that they are unsuitable for this task and would be used to monitor Indian air space. Ashley Tellis has argued that the Pakistani desire for the airborne warning systems is in fact a response to changes in the military balance with India and the increasing power of the Indian air force.[37] Other equipment from the United States, especially in the naval sphere, would also seem to have little to do with Afghanistan and rather to bear out India's fears.[38]

The claim by the leading Pakistani atomic scientist, Dr Abdel Qader Khan, in an interview published in March 1987,[39] that Pakistan had made nuclear weapons was subsequently denied, but the denial served merely to confirm a belief that had come to be widely held in both the West and India. The allegation complicated the efforts of the Reagan administration to get the new aid package through Congress in 1987–8. While India and its friends in Washington argued against military aid for a country which was making nuclear weapons, the administration argued that conventional military aid to Pakistan might encourage it not to make such weapons. (The official position of the administration was that Pakistan had the power to make nuclear weapons but had not yet done so.)[40] Soviet commentators have gone rather further than the Indians, claiming that Pakistan's nuclear ambitions have been 'encouraged by Washington'.[41] Although India and Pakistan have avoided full-scale war since 1971, there have been periods of tension along the extensive border. Disagreements over Kashmir and over the possible development of nuclear weapons are enhanced by Indian fears about American arms transfers to Pakistan and by Pakistan's view of India as being under 'Moscow's tutelage'.[42] Pakistan deploys most of its armed forces on the Indian border (and not near Afghanistan); and, similarly, most of India's military power is positioned against Pakistan (leaving – at the time of writing – only a small force along the Chinese border and the contingent in Sri Lanka). India claims that Sikh extremists are allowed to conduct terrorist operations from Pakistan, which borders on the Indian state of the Punjab. In October 1986, Rajiv Gandhi went as far as to accuse Pakistan of being involved in the attempt on his life.[43] In January 1987, alarm grew in Pakistan over India's 'Operation Brasstacks', in Rajasthan, near the border. Nearly one-third of the Indian army was involved, and although few in New Delhi believed that war would break out, it took a meeting between President Zia and Rajiv Gandhi (at Jaipur) to reduce the tension.[44] According to Indian military sources, Pakistani attacks on Indian positions in the Siachin glacier led to 24 Indian deaths in September 1987, and the 'very tense' situation was maintained as a result of another Pakistani incursion in January 1988.[45]

In such circumstances, it is not surprising that the possibility of improved relations between the Soviet Union and Pakistan should alarm India. The replacement in December 1986 of Babrak Karmal by Najibullah as General Secretary of the People's Democratic Party of Afghanistan led to hopes in Pakistan that the Soviet Union was moving seriously towards the withdrawal of its troops from Afghanistan. This was accompanied by renewed Soviet diplomatic activity. A London report in February 1987 that Moscow had told Islamabad that the Soviet Union could secure for Pakistan a no-war pact with India, in exchange for Pakistani cooperation in achieving a settlement in Afghanistan, was dismissed as 'speculative' by the Indian government. An article in *The Statesman* commented: 'It must offend our national self-esteem that anyone should have thought Moscow could not merely decide how India should order its relations with Pakistan but even tell the latter so.'[46] Pro-government forces in Pakistan noted India's concern. 'India had not taken kindly to Gorbachev's peace moves towards Pakistan, and in fact, these were upsetting of India's plans for this country.'[47]

The Soviet government, since the invasion of Afghanistan, has followed a carrot-and-stick policy towards Pakistan. On the one hand, it publicly denounced the Zia regime.[48] There were Soviet air attacks across the border from Afghanistan, causing considerable loss of life. Moscow expressed sympathy for the national aspirations of the Pashtuns (in the North-West Frontier Province) and the Baluchis, giving rise to fears that the Soviet Union might seek to create an independent Baluchistan and hence gain direct access via Afghanistan to the Indian Ocean.[49] At an Indo-Soviet seminar hosted by the Moscow IOS in October 1986, a Soviet participant wondered whether Pakistan might disintegrate, in view of the 'turmoil in Baluchistan'. The Indians responded that 'there need be no fear of Pakistani disintegration'.[50] In the early 1980s there was even a suggestion that the Soviet Union and India might jointly dismember Pakistan – a possibility that could be ruled out because of the high military, economic and political costs that such a move would entail for both parties.[51]

On the other hand, the USSR has taken care to ensure that its image in Pakistan was not purely negative. It has offered to meet Pakistan security interests by recognizing the Durand Line as the frontier between Afghanistan and Pakistan, in the context of an Afghan settlement. It has extended economic and technological aid for oil exploration, steel production and power generation. The *Pakistan and Gulf Economist* in November 1986 described economic relations with the Soviet Union as being 'of paramount importance to Pakistan'.[52] Several Karachi academics have called for Pakistan to settle its differences with the Soviet Union.[53] Mehrunissa Ali, for example, has argued that the United States cannot be considered a reliable ally for Pakistan.[54] Gorbachev's refusal during his 1986 visit to New Delhi to assert publicly that the Soviet Union would stand by India in a conflict with Pakistan (see Chapter 2) was naturally not welcome in India, but his expressed desire for friendship with both India and Pakistan, and for the peaceful settlement of disputes, was well received by Pakistani public opinion. This was a far cry from Kosygin's alleged encouragement to India in 1979 to 'teach Pakistan a lesson',[55] or Deputy Foreign Minister Kapitsa's 1985 promise to stand by India in a conflict.

The Afghanistan war brought serious problems to Pakistan. The most important was the presence of 3 million Afghan refugees, many of them armed. Drug-trafficking, bombing and sabotage by agents of the Kabul regime were widespread. Many Pakistanis believed that the United States was putting pressure on the government to prevent it achieving a settlement with Kabul in Moscow. The respected Karachi paper *Dawn* demanded in a leading article on 13 March 1987 that Pakistan should follow its national interests and make an agreement with the Soviet Union. 'Nothing should deflect it from this aim, certainly not transient considerations of how its posture on Afghanistan can affect prospects of economic and political aid on Capitol Hill.'[56] Similarly, Agha Shahi argued in a 1987 article that Pakistan's prime interest was in a quick settlement with Afghanistan, regardless of the American response. Such a settlement could lead to a radical improvement in Pakistani-Soviet relations. Shahi further affirmed that 'the Soviet Union has the undoubted potential to play a role in improving relations between Pakistan and India, as it did, for instance, in the Tashkent Conference in 1966'.[57]

Although the Soviet leaders would like to play such a role, this situation is, to say the least, a long way off. By early 1988 the Soviet leadership had agreed to withdraw the bulk of its forces from Afghanistan in the course of the following year. Brezhnev's attempts to impose a pro-Soviet government in Kabul had been defeated. Indians report having tried to persuade Soviet officials, by means of quiet diplomacy, of the need for a withdrawal from Afghanistan. While the main reason for Gorbachev's desire for a troop pullout was probably domestic political pressure, boosted by *glasnost*, the likely effect on Moscow's international standing played a major role. India would have conveyed to the Kremlin the damage that would be done to the USSR's prestige in the NAM if the occupation were to continue.

On 17 April 1988, Afghanistan and Pakistan signed the Geneva accords, which paved the way for a Soviet withdrawal. The details of the political wheeling and dealing which preceded the signing remain somewhat obscure. It appears that the Reagan administration (or at least its most influential members) had decided to meet the Soviet desire for a fig-leaf to cover the orderly retreat. It encouraged Pakistan to sign the accords and itself agreed to guarantee them. The Pakistani government of Prime Minister M.K. Junejo, as well as opposition politicians, favoured Washington's stance and the signing of an agreement with Kabul. General Zia, however, was more reluctant and wished to carry on giving full support to the Muja-hidin, who refused to recognize the Geneva process. Even after Zia's death, it does not seem likely that Pakistan's policy towards the Mujahidin will change significantly. Although Shevardnadze and Shultz acted as guarantors of the Geneva accords, it became clear that both Moscow and Washington were likely to continue render-ing military aid to their Afghan allies, even after the Soviet with-drawal, which began on 15 May. A Soviet withdrawal would undermine the justification given to the US Congress for aid to Pakistan, although a new justification might be found in relation to the Gulf. India could only welcome the Soviet decision.

The China factor

In the long term, as already noted, China is much more important to the Soviet Union than South or South-West Asia. This is not so much because of shared allegiance to Marxist-Leninist ideology as because of the sheer size of the Chinese population and the length of the Sino-Soviet and Sino-Mongolian border. Since the death of Mao, Soviet leaders have made repeated attempts to improve relations with Beijing, but with little result until the early 1980s. The election of the Reagan administration, with its anti-communist ideology and hard line on Taiwan, encouraged China to develop more evenly balanced relations with the superpowers. Other factors, such as common opposition to SDI and Congressional criticism of Chinese policy in Tibet,[58] also tended to push Beijing away from Washington and towards Moscow.

In general (at least since Gorbachev came to power) it has been the Soviet Union which has been keener to improve relations. Soviet commentators praised the adoption of a policy of 'no first use' of nuclear weapons by China (in 1967), well ahead of the Soviet Union (in 1982).[59] Gorbachev spoke at Vladivostok about the 'extremely responsible mission' of the 'two major socialist nations' in improv-ing security in Asia and the Pacific. His tone in regard to China was considerably warmer than in regard to the United States or Japan.[60]

Gorbachev's desire for a summit with Deng Xiaoping has been used by the Chinese to extract concessions. Of the 'three obstacles' seen by the Chinese as standing in the way of improved relations – the border, Afghanistan and Kampuchea – progress has been made on two. The Soviet government has made concessions on disputed rivers along the border. On Afghanistan, it had withdrawn over half its troops by late August 1988 and promised to withdraw the rest by February 1989. Beijing would probably be satisfied with any settlement acceptable to its Pakistani ally. On the problem of the presence of Vietnamese troops in Kampuchea, Moscow has said that this is a matter for Hanoi, but (as in Afghanistan) has promoted the concept of 'national reconciliation', to include all but representatives of the former Pol Pot regime. Sino-Soviet trade has increased dramatically, from $200 million in 1982 to $2.6 billion in 1986. A border incident in July 1986 did not affect the improvement in relations, and the following September Talyzin visited Beijing.[61] In February 1987 the two countries agreed to examine the whole length of the border.[62]

Relations between India and China generally improved in the course of the 1980s.[63] Nevertheless, as was clear at the time of Gorbachev's visit to New Delhi, there was concern in India about the rapprochement between Moscow and Beijing. Indians at the IOS seminar in October 1986 warned that China would be an unreliable partner for the Soviet Union, and expressed their anxiety about the future of Soviet support for India. The Soviet participants assured the Indians that they need have no worries.[64] Whereas in the past Moscow had been concerned about the improvement of Sino-Indian relations, now it was New Delhi that was concerned about the improvement of Sino-Soviet relations, and about the Soviet advice to India to improve its own relations with China. After Gorbachev's visit, Sino-Indian border tension increased. This followed the granting by India of full statehood to Arunachal Pradesh (formerly the North-East Frontier Agency) in the eastern sector of the disputed Sino-Indian border area.[65] The Chinese do not recognize the McMahon Line, agreed in 1914 between British India and Tibet, which India claims as its northern border. In May 1987 both sides reinforced their troops along the border, and clashes were reported in the region of Arunachal Pradesh. Moscow reportedly informed New Delhi that the Soviet priority was to maintain its improved relations with Beijing.[66] Soviet commentary took the line of trying to conciliate India and China.

It is not easy to explain the precise reasons for the border clashes of 1987. Although each side blamed the other, it would seem that neither could gain anything from an escalation of tension, except perhaps a stronger position at the border negotiations which were then approaching. Chinese suggestions that India was trying to force the Soviet Union to take a position in its favour, and that it therefore provoked the clashes, do not seem credible, since New Delhi was probably aware that Moscow would not back it, and since failure to get such support would weaken India's position. It is possible that the Indian government instigated the tension to distract attention from its domestic problems. Alternatively, China may have been provoked by the granting of statehood to Arunachal Pradesh. After tempers had cooled, a new round of border talks was held. This led to an improvement in relations and an agreement to reopen the consulates in Bombay and Shanghai, which had been closed after the 1962 Sino-Indian war.[67] This situation seems to suit Moscow quite well. As for India, public opinion generally favours a settlement with China on the basis of the status quo. It is at present difficult, however, to envisage the possibility of relations between Beijing and New Delhi improving to the point at which Moscow might begin to be concerned.

The nuclearization of South Asia

As outlined in Chapter 2, it was the Chinese nuclear weapons programme that encouraged India to seek its own nuclear weapons capability, which it demonstrated in the 1974 'peaceful nuclear explosion'. The Pakistan nuclear programme, in turn, was partly a response to the Indian developments. Prime Minister Bhutto's plans for an 'Islamic bomb', achieved with the help of Libyan finance and perhaps Chinese technical assistance, appear to have been realized under Zia. It is not entirely clear whether the Pakistan government wished the world to know that it had developed nuclear weapons, because this knowledge would deter potential attackers. It may be that Pakistan sees its bomb also as a counter to Indian conventional military superiority. It is easier to explain the denials of its nuclear capability. The future of the American aid programme would be questioned in Washington if Pakistan openly claimed that it was making nuclear weapons. Furthermore, the pressure in India to develop nuclear weapons would become difficult to resist. One of the prominent Indian hawks on nuclear weapons, K. Subrahmanyam, at the time the Director of the Institute for Defence Studies and Analyses in New Delhi, argued that India should recognize Pakistan's nuclear status and create its own programme.[68] Following the interview with A.Q. Khan in March 1987, the Indian Minister of

Defence, K.C. Pant, announced that India would review its nuclear policy, because of the 'emerging nuclear threat' from Pakistan.[69] The nuclearization of the Indian Ocean has also been cited as a reason for India to take that route.

There are several reasons why India is reluctant to develop nuclear weapons. There are fears that the United States would impose sanctions in retaliation. China would be alarmed by India's new status and India might actually become less secure in relation to its more powerful neighbour. Perhaps most important, for India to go nuclear would almost inevitably lead to a nuclear arms race between it and Pakistan. Raju Thomas goes so far as to say that the two countries 'are already engaged in a latent nuclear arms race'.[70] In the longer run an open arms race could only be resolved in India's favour, unless Pakistan were to achieve further substantial outside backing. Moreover, in any nuclear conflict, Pakistan would be more vulnerable than India because of its dependence on a single economic centre and port, Karachi.

India's rejection of the NPT is one of the points of difference between it and the Soviet Union. India argues that the NPT has done nothing to prevent the stockpiling of nuclear weapons by the countries which are allowed them, and that it discriminates against the other countries. Despite Soviet disapproval of the Pokhara explosion (see Chapter 2), Moscow agreed in 1976 to supply India with a large amount of heavy water. The 1977 International Atomic Energy Authority agreement on safeguards was applied to this sale and apparently also to a similar deal in 1980. These safeguards were 'stringent', but fell short of the 'full-scope safeguards' which the Soviet authorities professed to maintain – an indication that Moscow attached more importance to its friendship with India than to the fear of nuclear proliferation.[71] The Soviet Union has accused India of inconsistency, in attacking the production of weapons of mass destruction at meetings of the NAM but denouncing the NPT at the United Nations.[72] There is no evidence, it must be added, that India has already decided to produce nuclear weapons. Soviet acceptance of Indian assurances of the peaceful nature of its nuclear energy programme contrasts with increased Soviet condemnation of the Pakistani bomb.[73] The Soviet Union has, however, criticized India for voting against the proposal for a South Asian nuclear-weapon-free zone, while supporting proposals for such zones elsewhere.[74] India opposes the proposal because it would leave nuclear weapons in the hands of China.

The 'new political thinking' and the Asian context

The ideas promoted by Gorbachev about the interdependence of the world and the need to settle international disputes peacefully seem to have important consequences for Soviet policy towards India and its neighbours. Ideally, Moscow would like to have good relations with Afghanistan, Pakistan, India and China. This would be in the spirit of the Vladivostok speech. If Soviet troops are withdrawn completely from Afghanistan, it is likely that the overall level of tension in the region will decline. It is noteworthy that Gorbachev has failed to gain Indian support for his Vladivostok proposals (see Chapter 2).

The establishment of SAARC will prove to have been in the interests of the USSR if it provides a framework for a reduction of tension between India and Pakistan.[75] Soviet commentators have welcomed its formation and development.[76] The agreement signed in July 1987 by Rajiv Gandhi and President J.R. Jayawardene, on the entry of the Indian Peace-Keeping Force into Sri Lanka to end the activity of Tamil separatist groups, was also welcomed by Moscow. Prior to the agreement, Moscow had backed all the moves of India to aid the Tamil minority in Sri Lanka, including the airlifting of food and medicines, against the wishes of the Colombo government.[77] This was to be expected: Jayawardene's United National Party was traditionally close to America and Britain. When India decided to help Colombo by moving against the Tamil Tigers, Moscow backed Rajiv Gandhi's change in tactics.[78] The Indo-Sri Lankan agreement could legitimately be represented as a means of reducing international tension.

It has primarily been the American commitment to Pakistan that has driven India towards the Soviet Union in the 1980s. If US-Pakistani ties are reduced because of the Soviet withdrawal from Afghanistan, then India may become less dependent on the Soviet Union. The Soviet desire for better relations with China may leave the Soviet-Indian relationship ultimately unharmed, if Sino-Indian relations also improve, but it has already caused some strain. Sino-Soviet relations will never return to the position of the 1950s. China will not forget the economic damage which Khrushchev caused by withdrawing Soviet aid. The Soviet leadership will not give up significant areas of territory for the sake of good relations. As Robert Horn says, the 'deep-seated visceral fear of China does not incline the Kremlin to trust Peking's response to any concessions Moscow might make'.[79] It is likely that a deterioration in Indo-Pakistani or Sino-Soviet relations would encourage India or the USSR, respectively, to seek to enhance relations with the other. The overall experience of the period since 1971, and indeed before that, does suggest, however, that both sides see a long-term geopolitical rationale in maintaining close ties.

4

THE GLOBAL CONTEXT

This chapter attempts to examine the degree of influence exerted on each other by the Soviet Union and India in a wider context than the immediate Asian sphere just considered.

The Indian Ocean as a Zone of Peace

The question of the militarization of the Indian Ocean is one over which the interests of the Soviet Union and India appear to diverge, but on which India has succeeded in influencing the Soviet Union towards the adoption of its own position. The Soviet Union began to deploy ships in the Indian Ocean in 1968. This was part of Gorshkov's expansion of the Soviet navy into a global force. The Soviet Union's justification for its naval presence is that it is to counter the build-up of American ships and American submarines, which are capable of launching nuclear attacks on Soviet territory. The United States justifies its presence in terms of the need to prevent the Soviet Union from filling the vacuum left by the British withdrawal from the region. In response to the threat of a superpower arms race in the Indian Ocean, the NAM summit at Lusaka in 1970 proposed, with Indian support, that it be declared a 'Zone of Peace'. Military installations were to be removed, and forces were to be reduced to a level which did not threaten the states of the region. In October 1971 Sri Lanka moved this proposal at the UN General Assembly, again with Indian support. Both superpowers argued that the implementation of such a proposal would interfere with freedom of navigation, and abstained on the motion, which nevertheless was carried. Since then, the proposal has been regularly raised at the UN and the NAM, but attempts to convene a conference on the Indian Ocean have been thwarted.

At the General Assembly in November 1973 India again voted for the proposal, whereas both superpowers once more abstained. Moscow was unwilling to support a view that laid the blame for the militarization of the Indian Ocean equally on the two superpowers. During Brezhnev's visit to New Delhi later in the month, a compromise was reached. Both sides committed themselves to encouraging talks with the other states involved, with the ultimate aim of securing a Zone of Peace. Pakistan was unenthusiastic about the proposal, since in the absence of an American and indeed a Soviet presence, India would have domination of the Ocean. This was precisely one of the reasons why India was backing the idea – to exclude outside influence. A Pakistani observer has written: 'India's advocacy of the demilitarization of the Indian Ocean by the superpowers is an essential element of her goal to establish naval supremacy.'[1]

In 1977 the Carter administration proposed to the Soviet Union a plan for the complete demilitarization of the Indian Ocean. India welcomed this initiative, which effectively called the Soviet bluff. Negotiations began, but since the Soviet side was not really interested in withdrawing from the Indian Ocean, the agenda shifted towards freezing naval arms levels. The talks finally collapsed, however, in 1978. Thereafter a number of factors – the establishment of Carter's Rapid Deployment Force, the invasion of Afghanistan, which was seen by Washington as, among other things, a step towards Soviet acquisition of warm-water ports, and finally the creation of Reagan's CENTCOM – all helped to increase the militarization of the Indian Ocean.[2]

India has continued to demand a conference on the demilitarization of the Indian Ocean, and the Soviet Union has continued to give formal backing to India's wishes. Unlike the United States, the USSR has also supported India's proposal for a nuclear-weapon-free zone in the Indian Ocean. Some Indian analysts have come to see the Soviet nuclear presence as a reaction to the American presence,[3] while others see it in more aggressive terms, as linked to Soviet policy in Afghanistan and the Gulf.[4] The 41st session of the UN General Assembly in 1986 set a deadline of 1988 for the calling of the conference. Gorbachev, in his speech to the Indian parliament in November 1986, set out proposals for demilitarization which centred on the reduction of the military presence of outside powers (as opposed to that of the littoral states, such as India). Both he and Rajiv Gandhi implicitly blamed the United States for lack of progress towards this. The Soviet and Indian positions seemed to have converged completely; the logic of the 'new political thinking' would be that the Soviet Union had no interest in keeping forces in the Indian Ocean, provided that American forces were also absent. Moreover, the growth of the Indian navy meant that there was a friendly presence in the region.[5] In October 1987, responding to an Indian appeal, Gorbachev again backed the Peace Zone proposal and blamed the United States for halting the dialogue about it. On this occasion, however, he gave priority to reducing the naval activity of the littoral states.[6]

The non-aligned movement
As the Soviet-Indian relationship has developed, a major aim of the Soviet Union has been to secure Indian backing for Soviet positions in global forums. The support of India, the world's largest democracy and a country which (unlike Ethiopia, for instance) cannot be considered a mere Soviet client, is seen in Moscow as important for both practical and propaganda reasons. Such support has by no means always been forthcoming; I have already referred to India's abstentions over Afghanistan at the United Nations, and its refusal to endorse the Soviet proposals for a collective security system in Asia. Where there is a Soviet-Indian consensus, moreover, it is as likely to result from Indian influence on the Soviet Union as the other way around.

It would be wrong to suggest that India has acted as a surrogate for the Soviet Union in organizations which the latter is unable to join, such as the Commonwealth and the NAM. As a founding member of the NAM, India has always declared its opposition to racism, colonialism and the exploitation of the LDCs by Western companies and agencies. The ideas of Nehru and his successors owe more to a combination of nationalism and Fabianism than to Soviet Marxism. Interests come before non-alignment in the hierarchy of Indian foreign-policy influences, however, and New Delhi has normally muted its criticisms of Soviet actions, while regularly attacking the Americans. It is not difficult for the Soviet Union, with its anti-imperialist ideology and its lack of a history of Third World colonization, to present itself as the friend of the South against the North. Western economic involvement in South Africa allowed Soviet statements about the West as an ally of apartheid to find resonance in India, as in many other Third World countries. Far from the Soviet Union influencing India against apartheid, it was Gandhi who was fighting racism in South Africa even before the October Revolution. In the Middle East, the Soviet Union followed India's lead in recognizing the Palestine Liberation Organization. In Central America and the Caribbean, India does not follow the Soviet position, but it does have an ideological interest in opposing American interference in the region, irrespective of the impact on its relations with the United States. At the non-aligned summit in Havana in July 1979, the allies of the Soviet Union, headed by Cuba, which was chairing the movement, argued that the USSR and the socialist countries were the 'natural ally' of the non-aligned. This attempt to revise the basic principles of the NAM was fiercely resisted by Yugoslavia and by the caretaker government of India, led by Charan Singh.

Soviet and Indian interests did coincide, however, on the question of Kampuchea. The genocidal Pol Pot regime had been overthrown by means of a Vietnamese invasion. Vietnam was by now a Soviet ally, and also an ally of India against China. The Western powers continued to recognize Pol Pot. India argued at the NAM summit, and later at the United Nations, that Kampuchea's seat be left empty, rather than be held by Pol Pot or by the Heng Samrin regime installed by Vietnam. When Mrs Gandhi returned to power, she moved closer to the Soviet and Vietnamese positions and recognized Heng Samrin.

In February 1981 the NAM foreign ministers met in New Delhi. As part of the Soviet campaign to lobby India, which was chairing the meeting, to promote the idea of the socialist commonwealth as the natural ally of the non-aligned, the Soviet press carried articles recalling how the USSR had repeatedly stood by India in its hour of need. Moscow hoped that the ministers would avoid calling for a Soviet withdrawal from Afghanistan and a Vietnamese withdrawal from Kampuchea. Although the Indian draft declaration was closer to the Soviet position on the issues than previous Indian government statements, the ministers forced a compromise, calling for the withdrawal of unnamed foreign troops in both cases. Similarly, the final declaration on the Indian Ocean demanded that the (unnamed) 'great powers' reduce their naval presence.

In March 1983 New Delhi hosted the NAM summit. As at the foreign ministers' meeting, the main Soviet concerns were Afghanistan and Kampuchea. India prevented the former Cambodian leader, Prince Sihanouk, from addressing the summit, and Kampuchea's seat was left empty. India proposed a draft declaration which was seen by many of the participating delegations as driving the movement in a pro-Soviet direction on Afghanistan, Kampuchea and the Indian Ocean. In the course of the summit, India retreated, and the final statement called for the withdrawal of foreign troops from Afghanistan and Kampuchea and the resumption of negotiations on the Indian Ocean. It condemned the United States fifteen times and criticized the Soviet Union only twice. However, Moscow was reported to be dissatisfied with India's performance. Soviet diplomats had lobbied strongly to prevent the NAM taking a position hostile to the Soviet Union on Afghanistan. They had reminded India of past Soviet help, and made it clear that they now expected a return. In fact, the New Delhi meeting marked a shift from left to centre for the NAM. Soviet observers appear to have believed that India had yielded too easily to the attacks on the original draft.[7] Nevertheless, the US State Department described the declaration as 'in many respects an unbalanced and polemical document which does not reflect the principles of non-alignment'.[8]

It has been suggested that until the invasion of Afghanistan the Soviet link had advanced India's influence in the NAM.[9] Since then, some Indian observers admit, India has paid a political price for the connection and has sought to make plain its independence of Moscow.[10] It is not surprising that a Soviet analysis of the NAM, published in 1986, but probably written rather earlier, included India as one of the countries in the political centre of the NAM rather than on the left. These countries were described as having a progressive foreign policy course but being unwilling to 'openly confront with imperialism'.[11] A Soviet survey of India's work in chairing the non-aligned movement from 1983 to 1986, published in 1987, appeared to reflect the views of those in Moscow who wished to cultivate the more conservative Third World governments rather than the socialist and socialist-oriented regimes. It expressed uncritical support for India's policies on Asia, the Indian Ocean, Africa, the Middle East, Central America, world disarmament and North-

South relations. More significantly, Soviet recognition of India's role in the NAM came from the highest level – in Gorbachev's Vladivostok speech. 'The recognized leader of this movement is great India, with its moral authority and traditional wisdom, with its unique political experience and huge economic possibilities.'[12]

At the Harare summit of the NAM in September 1986, Rajiv Gandhi played the role of a unifier and consensus-builder. He called for a Soviet withdrawal from Afghanistan and an end to American interference in Nicaragua. In spite of criticisms made in the past of the Indian stance on Afghanistan, India was invited to chair the Afghanistan subcommittee. The meeting reaffirmed the basic positions of the 1983 New Delhi summit. Particular attention was given to developments in South Africa and to global nuclear disarmament. The latter issue has become so important in the Soviet-Indian relationship that it deserves separate treatment.[13]

Global nuclear disarmament
The non-aligned countries, from the time of Nehru, had always taken a stance against the ownership of nuclear weapons by the superpowers. With a few exceptions, the divisions among them over the NPT were related, not to the desire of countries to acquire their own nuclear weapon capabilities, but rather to the fact that the NPT appeared to seek to monopolize nuclear weapons for the depository states. India and other non-aligned countries opposed the NPT regime of safeguards against the proliferation of nuclear weapons. They resented 'the suggestion that they might clandestinely use civilian nuclear technology to make bombs . . . they feel that the aim of the nuclear "haves" in withholding their technology from them is to keep the developing countries in perpetual bondage.'[14]

Following NATO's 1979 'twin-track' decision on the deployment of intermediate nuclear weapons, the Soviet Union launched a worldwide campaign against Western nuclear policies. When, in March 1983, President Reagan made his 'Star Wars' speech, the Soviet leaders were seriously alarmed about the possible impact of the Strategic Defense Initiative (SDI) on their own defences and their economy. They stepped up the campaign against American nuclear weapons. This produced a positive response among Third World countries, which were concerned about the deteriorating international situation and also angry at the diversion into the arms race of resources that they felt were needed for development. India, which chaired the NAM from 1983 to 1986, played a major role in articulating these concerns, demanding a freeze on nuclear weapons and the halting of nuclear testing, and opposing the extension of the arms race into space. In January 1985 the leaders of India, Argentina, Greece, Sweden, Mexico and Tanzania – 'six nations from five continents' – met in New Delhi. The 'Delhi Six', under Rajiv Gandhi's leadership, issued a 'Delhi Declaration' embracing these demands.

In May 1985, two months after becoming General Secretary, Gorbachev commented that the Delhi Six and the USSR shared the same final objective, that of ridding the world of nuclear weapons. In August he announced a moratorium on nuclear testing. This was seen as an answer to the appeal of the Delhi Six. In April 1986, the NAM foreign ministers met in New Delhi to prepare for the forthcoming summit. The mood was strongly anti-Washington, since the meeting immediately followed the American bombing of civilians in Libya. The foreign ministers passed a political declaration, drafted by India, welcoming Gorbachev's speech of 15 January 1986 in which he outlined proposals for a nuclear-weapon-free world by the year 2000. The IOS annual on India gave credit to New Delhi for successfully resisting the attempt of the right wing of the NAM to adopt a less pro-Soviet position.[15] When the leaders of the Delhi Six met in Ixtapa in August 1986 to review progress since the Delhi Declaration, Rajiv Gandhi made this comment on Soviet policy: 'In response to our call, the Soviet Union unilaterally accepted a moratorium on nuclear tests and twice extended it. We commend them and deeply appreciate the earnestness they have shown.'[16] The Harare summit in September 1986 gave full backing to the proposals of the Delhi Six. It issued the Harare Appeal for Peace and Disarmament, which was warmly welcomed by Gorbachev.[17]

In November 1986, during the General Secretary's visit to India, Rajiv Gandhi identified himself even more closely with the Soviet position by signing the new 'Delhi Declaration' with the Soviet leader. Although the Indian side could claim that this declaration committed Gorbachev to the Gandhian principle of non-violence, in the real political world it amounted to an uncritical endorsement of the Soviet position at nuclear arms control and disarmament negotiations. The document proposed the calling of a convention to ban the use or threat of use of nuclear weapons, the prohibition of nuclear weapons tests, the banning of nuclear weapons from space and the destruction of all nuclear weapons by the year 2000. It further called for a ban on chemical weapons and a reduction in conventional arms. The Delhi Declaration has been widely used in Soviet propaganda as an example of the 'new political thinking' and of the convergence of Soviet and Indian ideas on international issues. Indeed, Gorbachev was still referring to it at the CPSU Conference in June 1988: 'We, for our part, have got the chance . . . of extracting whatever is useful from ideas originating in other cultures and spiritual traditions, as was reflected, for example, in the 1986 Delhi Declaration.'[18]

It has been suggested that Rajiv Gandhi's alignment with the Soviet Union on global disarmament is an attempt to pacify his left wing, whereas his real intention is to improve relations with the West. If this was in fact the case, the tactic has been counterproductive. Circles within the United States which are suspicious of India see confirmation of their fears in documents such as the Gorbachev-Gandhi Delhi Declaration, and argue against the export of technology to India. The fact that the Delhi Declaration is in line with the positions of the Delhi Six and the NAM majority is evidence that the stance of the Indian government reflects a major trend in the thinking of the Third World (and of the peace movement of the developed world). The Indian government has obviously been prepared to express its solidarity with the Soviet Union on global security, even at the cost of being denied some American technology.

Within months of the Delhi Declaration, however, the Soviet Union resumed nuclear testing, pointing to the failure of the Americans to institute a moratorium of their own. This move showed the limits of Moscow's willingness to follow the wishes of India and other friendly states when Soviet decision-makers perceived that their own country's security was at stake.

The Soviet-Indian relationship and the West

Some specialists have argued that the Soviet-Indian relationship will lose its intensity as India's economic development requires closer ties with the capitalist world. Harish Kapur, for example, has argued that India's need to interact with the outside world 'will accelerate. But this will not be with the Soviet Union. The new pattern of its economic needs will probably push India to seek more links with Western Europe and Japan.'[19] Roger Kanet agrees that the USSR's 'relevance for India's interests and concerns is likely to wane'.[20] These concerns are considered in Chapter 5. When Rajiv Gandhi came to power, there were hopes in the West that he might introduce a fresh perspective on India's foreign relations. But, as Leo Rose put it: 'Speculation that ... Gandhi might be interested in eliminating the pro-Soviet tilt in Indian foreign policy has been based in large part on wishful thinking.'[21]

Quite apart from India's shortage of hard currency, there are political obstacles to a weakening of the country's links with the Soviet Union and to a move towards the West. India's stance on North-South issues leads it to be critical of many Western policies, and especially of attempts to export the ideology of the free market. The activities of Sikh extremists in the United States, Britain and Canada was, for a time, an important issue in India's relations with these countries. Moves towards an extradition treaty with Britain have cleared a major obstacle to the improvement of bilateral relations. South Africa, however, still remains an important issue. When the British Prime Minister, Margaret Thatcher, used the Commonwealth summit of October 1987 to denounce the African National Congress as 'terrorists', the action confirmed Indian suspicions that Britain and other countries were not prepared to hurt themselves to remove apartheid. Rajiv Gandhi even suggested that Britain under Mrs Thatcher had given up the moral leadership of the Commonwealth. *The Hindu* of Madras wrote that 'countries such as Britain are more interested in holding on to their economic and financial ties to Pretoria and are merely paying lip service to ending racial discrimination'.[22] Nevertheless, despite those criticisms, India buys arms from West European countries and generally enjoys good relations with most of the capitalist world.

It is the relationship with the United States which is the most complicated for India. In August 1986, Rajiv Gandhi hinted at American backing for Sikh terrorists, and linked this backing with India's protest against the bombing of Libya. He also referred to the American pressure on India which had been exerted at the time of Mrs Gandhi's attack on the American invasion of Grenada.[23] The principal problem, however, is American military aid to Pakistan, including the supply of F-16s, which might be used to drop nuclear bombs on India.[24]

American efforts to sell India weapons were continued under the Reagan administration. The unwillingness of the Americans to allow licensed production of tanks or aircraft seems to be the chief obstacle to their success. The problem has been with the State Department and the Pentagon rather than with the manufacturers.[25] Even if the significant defence contracts were signed, however, it is hardly likely that the United States could displace the Soviet Union as India's principal supplier. Since 1984 the Reagan administration has become more aware of India's regional importance and more willing to consider technology transfer. Although this has not yet had an impact on arms sales, it has eased conditions on the civilian side. For some time India has been interested in buying a Cray super-computer, primarily for forecasting monsoons. By the end of 1987 Pentagon opposition had been overcome and the sale went ahead, though India was not allowed to acquire the most advanced model, which it had wanted. However far economic links develop between India and the West, it seems unlikely that they will lead to a major change in India's political and defence links with the Soviet Union.[26]

5

SOVIET ECONOMIC AND MILITARY INVOLVEMENT

The Soviet Union's involvement in India's defence is expressed primarily in the export of arms. Since India's capacity to pay for these arms, and the price at which the Soviet Union delivers them, are directly linked to the economic relationship between the two countries (one in which, as we shall see, the Soviet Union seems, effectively, to subsidize the Indian economy), these two aspects of the relationship are best investigated together.

The evolution of the economic relationship

The construction of the Bhilai steel plant, agreed in 1955, was the first major Soviet aid project in India. By the end of 1987, over 70 such schemes had been completed. According to Soviet estimates, they accounted for the production of 36% of India's steel, 32% of its aluminium, 77% of its metallurgical equipment, 47% of its power equipment, 43% of its mining equipment and 10% of its power. Another 40 schemes were being designed or constructed.[1] Naturally, as India's own industrial base and skilled labour force grew, the Soviet share in these projects declined. Soviet economic aid has been concentrated on developing the basic industries in the state sector, sometimes with an orientation towards the Soviet market. Soviet officials argue that whereas American aid was designed to bring India into the American sphere of influence, Soviet aid was designed to help it strengthen its economy and ultimately achieve real economic independence. Indians themselves have noted that

69

whereas American aid was directed mainly towards consumption, Soviet aid was intended to increase production.[2] The Soviet Union has avoided direct investment in India, presumably to be able to make propaganda points about the difference between socialist and capitalist aid. It is not always easy to distinguish aid from trade, since aid can be concealed as trade through favourable pricing policies (or alternatively be offset through unfavourable pricing). Soviet-Indian commerce takes place within a framework of trade agreements, which since 1953 have normally been made for a five-year period.[3] Since the second five-year agreement, concluded in 1958, no foreign exchange has been used. That agreement took account of India's balance-of-payments crisis and laid down that trade balances would be settled in rupees rather than hard currency. Further, Soviet loans could be repaid through the export of goods.

In the years that followed, Soviet-Indian trade increased dramatically, albeit from a low base. In 1955–6 the figures for the Soviet share in India's exports and imports were both less than one per cent. By 1974–5 the Soviet share of India's imports had risen to 9%, and of its exports to 12%, having peaked in 1972–3 at 15.5%. At that time the USSR was India's top export market.[4]

Soviet-Indian cooperation expanded after the Bangladesh war; 40 agreements on economic, technological, scientific and cultural cooperation were signed between 1972 and 1974. During the visit of Planning Minister D.P. Dhar to Moscow in September 1972, he finalized an agreement to establish an 'Intergovernmental Soviet-Indian Commission on Economic, Scientific and Technical Cooperation'. This commission's first annual meeting took place in February 1973 in New Delhi. Ambitious plans for trade, aid and economic cooperation were adopted, and the two countries discussed coordination of their five-year plans.

A particular area of cooperation covered in these agreements was joint production: the Soviet Union would export raw materials to Indian industry and then reimport the finished products. Nevertheless, the Soviet share of Indian trade deteriorated in the mid-1970s. It was in order to demonstrate the importance it attached to its relationship with New Delhi that Moscow agreed in 1976, after rejecting earlier Indian requests, to sell crude oil to India, thereby forgoing valuable hard-currency earnings (at the same time as telling the East Europeans to look elsewhere to satisfy their increasing needs).[5] The agreement on cooperation up to 1990, signed during

Kosygin's 1979 visit to New Delhi, included provision for 'compensation' deals, whereby the Soviet Union would construct plants in India and receive payment in the form of the goods produced. During Arkhipov's visit the following year, it was decided that in future the Indian private sector could be involved in cooperation projects. Specific 'compensation' projects were agreed during Brezhnev's visit at the end of 1980, in a package of Soviet aid worth over 40 billion rupees. Further, Moscow agreed to increase oil exports, even though it was curtailing them to Eastern Europe owing to increasing difficulties in the Soviet oil-extraction industry. The effect of this trade expansion was that in 1981, for the first time, the Soviet Union overtook the United States as India's largest trading partner.

Soviet and Western economic aid

In comparison with the advanced capitalist countries, the Soviet Union has not been a major donor of economic aid to the LDCs, not even to India. It has sought to place responsibility for the backwardness of the Third World on imperialist exploitation. Despite its backing for the claims of the 'South' against the 'North', it has, at least until recently, refused to see itself as part of the 'North'. The OECD estimated Soviet economic assistance in 1985 as 0.28% of GNP. The bulk of this goes to LDC members of the Council for Mutual Economic Assistance – Vietnam, Cuba and Outer Mongolia. In 1984–5 these received 65% of total CMEA aid (85% of which comes from the USSR), excluding scholarships, while most of the rest goes to other communist LDCs, and to Ethiopia, Nicaragua and countries of 'socialist orientation'. India's share was 3% – the same as those of Kampuchea and the People's Democratic Republic of Yemen.[6]

The CIA figures of Soviet economic aid to the LDCs appear to exclude the major communist recipients and also most of the minor ones (although, rather confusingly, Afghanistan is included). This makes it difficult to discern the overall priority given to India in comparison with the communist countries. According to the CIA, over the whole period between 1954 and 1984, India was the second largest recipient of Soviet economic aid, after Turkey. In 1985, however, India overtook Turkey in terms of the aggregate of aid received since 1954, with $4,422 million (against Turkey's $3,399 million) out of a total $32,916 million. Interestingly, while India received no aid in 1984 (out of a total $2,482 million), in 1985 it received $1,200 million out of $2,390 million – half of the total amount for that year. Although aid figures fluctuate from one year to the next, it is clear that up to 1985, at least, Soviet policy-makers were involved in what to them was a major economic aid commitment to India.[7]

Western aid to India is subject to similar fluctuations. Figures issued by the UN Conference on Trade and Development (UNCTAD) relating to official development assistance (oda) for the OECD Development Assistance Committee (DAC) countries show that over the period 1979–83, oda to India reached a high of $931 million in 1981 and a low of $471 million in 1982.[8] Leaving aside the exceptional year 1985, the aggregate of Western economic aid to India dwarfs that provided the Soviet Union. This impression is confirmed by Indian figures of sources of external assistance. Comparisons between the Soviet Union and individual Western countries are misleading to the point of meaninglessness here, since much Western aid is channelled through multilateral organizations such as the International Bank for Reconstruction and Development (IBRD), the International Development Agency (IDA) and the Aid-India Consortium. The Soviet Union was responsible for 4.9% of the cumulative total aid authorized for India up to March 1985 (compared with 27.0% authorized by the IDA, 14.2% by the IBRD, 15.2% by the USA, 9.6% by the UK, 4.8% by the FRG, 3.8% by Canada and 3.2% by Japan).[9]

Such calculations are rendered more complex and less reliable by fluctuations in the dollar-rupee exchange rate over the period, and the inherent difficulties of cross-temporal comparisons under inflationary conditions. A further problem is that aid authorized is not always dispersed. At certain periods this has been a particular feature of Soviet aid. This is because Soviet aid is more often for long-term projects, in which the Soviet equipment may be delivered towards the end of a long period of construction. By March 1985, however, the proportion of undispersed Soviet credits to total authorized credits was comparable with that of Western countries and agencies, but the subsequent aid packages may well revive the disparity. Also important is the form of the aid. Outright grants from the Soviet Union have been very small and apparently zero from 1980–1 to 1983–4; Britain accounts for over half the grants utilized in this period.[10] Soviet aid takes the form of loans, which, although described in some Indian sources as being repayable in foreign currencies,[11] are perhaps more accurately described as payable through the export of goods.[12] These figures again show the Soviet Union as a relatively small supplier of aid.

A particularly telling point about Soviet aid is that in every year from 1967 to 1981, with the exception of 1973, the total of aid and interest repayments to the USSR was greater than the total of aid disbursed to India. From 1982 the flow of funds was in India's favour, since the Soviet Union was financing a steel works at Visakhapatnam. This flow of funds from an LDC to the USSR appears incongruous when set against Soviet accusations about imperialist exploitation of the Third World, but it is found also in relation to Egypt, Iran, Iraq and Turkey.[13]

It is often claimed by Soviet and Indian commentators, however, that it was the Soviet willingness to provide aid which initially encouraged the Western countries to move in, and then impelled them to offer better terms than they would otherwise have done in the absence of Soviet proposals. This view is supported by the high level of Soviet loan authorizations in the period 1956–61, amounting to about 30% of the total available to India. After this the level of Soviet authorizations fell as the level of Western authorizations increased significantly.[14]

Patterns and problems in Soviet-Indian trade

Patterns of Soviet-Indian trade are hard to analyse because the published statistics are misleading, in that they omit Soviet arms transfers. This omission may have the effect of making a Soviet trade surplus appear as an Indian one.

If one examines the change in the level of Soviet-Indian trade over the whole period from the Bangladesh war to the present, it appears that there has been a dramatic increase. Between 1970 and 1985 the level rose about sevenfold measured in dollars, eightfold measured in roubles and elevenfold measured in rupees.[15] The Soviet and Indian figures tell a broadly similar story (see Tables 1 and 2). The expansion of the value of trade – in both directions – that occurred steadily through the 1970s gained an extra impetus between 1979 and 1981. Over this period India was almost continuously in surplus, which was one of the factors behind the sudden Soviet unilateral decision in 1983 to cancel a wide range of Indian imports. This enabled the Soviet Union to move into surplus for a while, until 1986, when the impact of the fall in the price of Soviet oil brought its account again into deficit, despite a substantial reduction in Soviet imports. In 1987 the trade was in balance at a total level of about 2.2 billion roubles.

These figures, however, undoubtedly give a misleading account of the real volume of trade, since they conceal the effects of the repeated increases in the price of oil and oil products. Trade in this category was not important until 1974, when the volume of Soviet exports slightly more than doubled but the value increased sixfold. The share of oil and oil products in Soviet exports therefore increased from 5% of the value in 1973 to 25% in 1974. This trend increased so that in 1977 oil and oil products accounted for over half of Soviet exports, and peaked in 1982 at 78%. By 1986 the fall in oil prices had brought the share down to 42%.[16] By contrast, the share of equipment in Soviet exports to India in some years fell below 10%. Indian exports to the Soviet Union have also been dominated by food and raw materials, especially tea and coffee, and by textiles, but consumer goods and manufacturing equipment are increasing in importance.

The structure of Soviet exports to India actually reflects the global trading position of the USSR, as a supplier of raw materials to the world. The fact that this position has been repeated in relation to a Third World country such as India has considerably irritated Soviet foreign-trade officials. They have gone on trying to persuade India to increase the level of capital equipment purchases from the USSR. They have, however, encountered resistance because India on the whole prefers to obtain technology from the West and Japan rather than suffer the disadvantage of Soviet technological backwardness. The 1983 Soviet cancellations of imports seem to have been mainly a form of retaliation or pressure on the Indians for their lack of interest in Soviet equipment. The move caused considerable disruption and a degree of unemployment, particularly where factories had been established to supply the Soviet market and in areas which had become dependent on Soviet demand, such as the cashew-nut industry in Kerala. Some of the import cutbacks were reversed, after Indian protests, and Indian equipment purchases have since been increased.

Table 1 Soviet–Indian trade: Soviet statistics – million roubles

Year	Soviet import	Soviet export	Soviet Ex − Im	Total	% of Soviet trade
1987	1072.6	1105.4	+ 32.8	2178.0	1.7
1986	1233.6	957.8	− 275.8	2191.2	1.7
1985	1509.5	1574.9	+ 65.4	3084.4	2.2
1984	1272.0	1537.5	+ 265.5	2809.5	2.0
1983	1051.0	1271.6	+ 220.6	2322.6	1.8
1982	1473.8	1040.2	− 433.6	2514.0	2.1
1981	1333.8	1064.1	− 269.7	2397.9	2.2
1980	878.6	861.2	− 17.4	1739.8	1.8
1979	510.0	525.1	+ 15.1	1035.1	1.3
1978	407.3	364.1	− 43.2	771.4	1.1
1977	565.2	360.8	− 204.4	926.0	1.5
1976	376.5	271.0	− 105.5	647.5	1.1
1975	393.5	292.1	− 101.4	685.6	1.4
1970	242.6	122.3	− 120.3	364.9	1.7

Source: Ministerstvo vneshnei torgovli, *Vneshniaia torgovlia SSSR v 1986g*, and earlier volumes; *Vneshniaia torgovlia*, 1988, no. 3, supplement.

Table 2 India's trade with the USSR and the USA compared: Indian statistics – crores of rupees (one crore = 10 million)

| Year | India–USSR | | | | India–USA | | |
	Indian export	Indian import	Indian Ex − Im	Total	Indian export	Indian import	Total
1985–86	1937.0	1673.0	+ 264.0	3610.0	1994.0	2086.0	4080.0
1984–85	1654.6	1803.4	− 148.8	3458.0	1768.5	1666.6	3435.1
1983–84	1305.9	1658.6	− 352.7	2964.5	1396.6	1790.9	3187.5
1982–83	1662.1	1413.2	+ 248.7	3075.3	927.2	1426.5	2353.7
1981–82	1659.9	1136.9	+ 523.0	2796.8	919.6	1419.7	2339.3
1980–81	1225.7	1013.7	+ 212.0	2239.4	739.4	1518.6	2258.0
1979–80	638.1	822.3	− 184.2	1460.4	805.7	926.1	1731.8
1978–79	411.4	469.1	− 57.7	880.5	771.1	761.9	1533.0
1977–78	656.7	442.4	+ 214.3	1099.1	675.1	755.9	1431.0
1976–77	440.4	307.2	+ 133.2	747.6	547.2	1065.5	1612.7
1975–76	412.8	295.8	+ 117.0	708.6	505.4	1269.9	1775.3
1970–71	209.8	106.1	+ 103.7	315.9	206.8	453.0	659.8

Source: Indian Ministry of Planning, Central Statistical Office, *Statistical Pocket Book India 1985*; and *Statistical Abstract India 1984*, and earlier volumes.

In 1987 India accounted for 1.7% of all Soviet trade, by far the highest share of any non-socialist developing country (see Table 1). (Coincidentally, this was the same share India had held in 1970.) This still put it behind the FRG, France, Finland and Italy. The Soviet Union's importance for India was naturally larger than the other way round: in 1984–5 the Soviet Union was the source of 10.5% of India's imports and the destination of 14.3% of its exports.[17] It is when one compares the figures for Indo-Soviet trade with those for Indo-American trade (see Table 2) that one sees the expansion of the former in a more realistic perspective. Undeniably the Soviet trade has grown faster, in rupee terms; but the USA has been ahead of the USSR in total turnover in every year except 1981–2, 1982–3 and 1984–5.

The Soviet-Indian arrangements to avoid the use of hard currency in trade are paralleled in Soviet agreements with Afghanistan, Bangladesh, Egypt, Iran, Pakistan and Syria. These continue even though the USSR now insists that some exports to CMEA members, such as oil to Hungary, are paid for in hard currency. In dealing with LDCs, the Soviet Union appears to allow its trading partner to decide whether foreign exchange or soft currency is used.

The rouble-rupee agreement is trade-creating rather than trade-diverting, and works to the advantage of both sides. Neither is required to spend scarce foreign currency on imports from the other. In the 1960s there was some concern in India about reports that the Soviet Union was reselling for hard currency goods received from India, which led to allegations of exploitation. These views do not command support today. The agreement allows both countries to supply goods which, in a world of protectionist trading blocs, will not find markets elsewhere, often because of their low quality. It allows the Soviet Union to buy consumer goods it could otherwise not afford. The Indians gain oil without spending foreign currency. And although the Soviet Union forgoes hard currency by supplying this oil to India, or even spends money buying it from Iran to resell to India, it appears to see a political advantage in this.

Despite moves in both countries towards liberalizing foreign trade, it seems likely that the rouble-rupee arrangement will remain in place. In the past, the USSR has used its hard-currency surplus from trade with LDCs to buy advanced Western technology. India, however, has normally been in surplus in its trade with the USSR, and Moscow is unlikely to want this surplus to be converted into hard currency. India's preference is affected by its adverse experiences of abolishing the soft-currency arrangements it had with Yugoslavia, Hungary and Bulgaria. The rouble-rupee rate of exchange used in bilateral trade is not published, but India seems to fare no worse in its terms of trade with the Soviet Union than in its trade with the West. Indeed, the Soviet side reportedly tried during the Gorbachev visit to devalue the rupee against the rouble, without success. Perhaps the decisive factor, however, is that the rouble-rupee arrangement allows India to buy arms from the Soviet Union without spending hard currency.[18]

Unfortunately, the published statistics for Soviet-Indian trade do not include defence sales. These sales are normally financed by Soviet credits, which are then repaid through Indian exports to the USSR. These non-military exports do, however, appear in the figures. This creates the impression that the Indian trade surplus is much bigger than it really is.[19] Indeed, it has been claimed that if arms transfers are included, the Soviet Union has always had a trade surplus with India.[20]

Economic perspectives

Both India and the Soviet Union appear to see trade as useful in itself, for political reasons. The serious deterioration in the USSR's own terms of trade, brought about by the decline in the price of oil, and the consequent decline in the Soviet ability to import, gave added impetus to efforts to seek new forms of economic cooperation in the mid-1980s. India has increased its purchases of equipment from the Soviet Union, and this tendency is being promoted by the Soviet credits of one billion roubles agreed in 1985 and a further 1.5 billion in 1986. These credits are mainly aimed at the Indian public sector. As the focus of Indian government concern has shifted from heavy industry, which has traditionally benefited from Soviet aid, towards developing energy resources, so Soviet interest too has moved in this direction. The 1986 agreements cover the construction of a 2,400 MW hydroelectric power station in Tehri, modernization of the Bokaro steel works, the establishment of coal mines in Jharia and onshore oil exploration in West Bengal.[21] The Soviet Union will supply documentation, technical expertise and equipment, on a turnkey basis.

Much more is to be done if the target of increasing trade two-and-a-half times between 1986 and 1992 is to be met. The reputation of

Soviet aid to India is not unblemished. There are often problems with the lack of spare parts and after-sales service, but where Soviet technicians have remained in place after completed projects have been handed over to India, as at Bhilai, substantial success has been achieved. Opinions are divided over the reliability of Soviet buyers as regular customers.[22] The Barauni oil refinery, which could process neither Indian nor Gulf oil, and the Surgical Instrument Factory in Madras, which was reduced to making cutlery, are among the examples of Soviet-built plants which have proved unsuccessful. The compensation projects promised in 1980 have been slow to appear.

There are some areas, however, in which the Soviet Union is a world leader, and since Gorbachev's 1986 visit both sides have gone to considerable lengths to establish areas of cooperation. An Indo-Soviet Investment Centre has been opened in New Delhi. In 1987, in the conditions of *glasnost*, Soviet commentators felt able to criticize openly the structure of Soviet-Indian trade, and report that steps were being taken to diversify Soviet exports away from the concentration on raw materials towards machinery and equipment.[23] Guri Marchuk, President of the USSR Academy of Sciences, visited New Delhi in the spring at the head of a delegation of scientists and technologists, in an effort to identify areas of Soviet expertise which would benefit the Indian economy.[24] This was followed by the signing, during Rajiv Gandhi's visit to Moscow in July 1987, of a thirteen-year agreement on science and technology. The principal areas covered were biotechnology, laser and space science, electronics, computers and water prospecting. A Joint Council on Science and Technology was established.[25]

This cooperation is by no means a one-way flow from the Soviet Union to India. The Indian private sector has been supplying computers and software to the Soviet Union and is seeking to expand in this direction. Already, Western companies have established subsidiaries in India with the aim of achieving easier access to the Soviet market. Rank Xerox has been successfully selling photocopiers which have been assembled in India to the USSR, and this precedent is being built on. The advantage to Moscow is that it acquires Western technology without spending hard currency.

By the end of 1987 the Soviet Union had extended credits for an oil refinery at Karnal and a 500 MW thermal power station. More contentious in India was the Soviet resurrection of the offer, first made to the Janata government, to build a 1,000 MW nuclear power station. It appeared that India was considering the project favourably.[26] At the same time there were signs that the beginnings of the radical reform of the Soviet economy were attracting the interest of the Indian private sector. Soviet foreign-trade officials around the world have been heavily selling the idea of joint ventures. Indian private firms and Soviet enterprises have made a wide range of proposals. These include the production of Lada cars in South India, and joint production of footwear, motor components, road-building equipment, turbo-hydro generators, X-ray apparatus, ventilators, welding equipment and colour televisions in India, the Soviet Union or both. At the start of 1988, some thirty Indian state and private companies had submitted schemes for joint ventures with the Soviet Union. Ten projects for hotels and other construction schemes to be built in the USSR by Indian firms, and 125 co-production projects, were under consideration. Indians were complaining that despite (or perhaps because of) *perestroika*, Soviet officials were slow to clear the projects. A further problem was the lack of market research among Soviet customers.[27]

The defence relationship

India is currently dependent on the Soviet Union for around 60–65% of its arms imports. The total value of military sales is not published and is difficult to estimate, and in any case may be misleading because of the unquantifiable element of subsidy. It has been suggested that the total is not more than 15% of the aggregate of Soviet-Indian trade.[28] The CIA estimates the total value of Soviet arms transfers to India for 1981–5 as $4,200 million, or 69%, of a total $6,070 million of Indian arms imports.[29] Indian sources report the present proportion to be rather lower. This degree of dependence in itself makes India's link with the USSR strategically important, quite apart from any military or diplomatic support India might receive from Moscow in a conflict.

India has chosen to rely on Soviet equipment to this extent for a number of reasons. Soviet ships, aircraft and tanks have been relatively cheap in comparison with those made in the West, perhaps 40–50% lower in price,[30] and have often made up for their lack of technological sophistication by their robustness and reliability. Further, the credit terms available from the Soviet Union amount to a form of subsidy; and, moreover, under the trade arrangements, the credits are repaid in goods rather than in hard currency. Also important is the willingness of the Soviet suppliers – like the West Europeans but unlike the Americans – to allow India to produce under licence weapons of Soviet design. This accommodates India's desire to develop its own weapons industries. The country is now able to produce about two-thirds of its arms domestically. Additionally, Soviet military technology tends to develop cumulatively and to be compatible with previous generations. This makes it possible to upgrade licensed production facilities as improvements are made, whereas West European licences often require the construction of completely new production lines for new models of weapons.

The Soviet Union regards the supply of arms as a way of building political influence, and sees its interests being served by strengthening India. It is clear that it is sufficiently confident of its long-term position in India, and of the likelihood that the two countries will continue to perceive a convergence of their geopolitical interests, to risk sharing some of the latest military technology with the Indians. Although the agreements for licensed production began as long ago as 1962, the Soviet Union has still not extended the sharing of military know-how to more than a handful of countries. A further benefit to the USSR is that Indian purchases keep Soviet production lines running and enable costs to be kept down.[31]

In the 1950s India bought most of its arms imports from Britain. In the early 1960s, however, Britain, the United States and France expressed unwillingness to meet certain Indian requests, apparently doubting India's ability to handle particular naval weapons, and declined to offer credits. The United States refused to supply F-104 Starfighters and C-130 transport aircraft. In 1964 the Soviet Union, on the other hand, which had been selling India limited quantities of arms since 1960, offered it defence loans for ten years at 2% interest. India turned to the Soviet Union not only because of the cheapness of these credits but also because of its desire to acquire symbolic support against China, and to counter the American supply of supersonic Starfighters to Pakistan. According to Nihal Singh, only the Soviet Union seemed sympathetic to India's wish to become a strong military power with its own defence industry. The Soviet willingness to continue deliveries to India during the 1965 war with Pakistan contrasted with the American suspension of military equipment. Thereafter, India depended heavily on the Soviet Union: over the period 1967–77, to the tune of 81% of its arms imports.[32]

Despite the Soviet support for India in the Bangladesh war, in the mid-1970s Indira Gandhi began moves to diversify the sources of arms imports. This was perhaps not only to widen the options open to India, but also to seek better terms from the Soviet suppliers. Mrs Gandhi began negotiations to buy the Anglo-French Jaguar deep-penetration strike aircraft, which had a longer range than the Soviet MiG-23 on offer. The Janata government successfully concluded the Jaguar deal. In response, the Soviet side tried to make its weapons more attractive to India. In May 1980, after Indira Gandhi returned to power, a $1,630 million credit for India, repayable over fifteen years at 2.5% interest, was agreed in Moscow. This was for the purchase of MiG-25 Foxbat aircraft, fast-attack boats and T-72 tanks. These last were also to be produced under licence in India. A Pakistani source puts the value of this deal at between $8 and $10 billion at Western prices.[33] There seems to have been little Soviet competition against the West German submarines or the British Harrier jump-jets and Sea King helicopters which Mrs Gandhi bought after returning to power. Of greater significance was the decision to buy French Mirage-2000 fighters (partly taken to counter the F-16s sold by the United States to Pakistan, which could reach over half the Indian territory).

The Mirage purchase alarmed the Soviet leaders, and led to their sending to New Delhi, in March 1982, a delegation headed by Ustinov. He reportedly offered the T-82 tank and licensed production of the MiG-27 ground-attack fighters, with the aim of trying to persuade India to drop the Mirage deal. The Indian decision nevertheless to go ahead with Mirage did not lead Moscow to give up. In June 1983 Soviet officials showed Defence Minister Ramaswamy Venkataraman plans for the MiG-29 Fulcrum and MiG-31 Foxhound, which they said would perform better than the F-16 and F-15. They also offered improved versions of the T-72 and T-80 tanks. At the same time, by a combination of diplomatic pressure (of which the cancellation of imports from India may have been a part), low prices and easy credit, they sought to stop India from buying machine-guns, TOW missiles and howitzers from the United States. Secretary Shultz visited New Delhi in July 1983 and expressed American willingness to sell weapons to India. But the Soviet efforts paid off. Indira Gandhi came round to the decision to scrap the part of the Mirage deal relating to licensed production, and to have the MiGs instead. The Indian Defence and Foreign Ministers made visits to Moscow in June and September, and a contract was agreed concerning MiGs (even before the MiG-29 had entered the service of the Warsaw Pact allies) and T-80 tanks. The value of this deal was reported as nearly $3 billion.[34] The MiG-31s would be entering service with India almost as soon as they would with the Soviet air forces – an unprecedented situation for Soviet arms transfers. The visit to New Delhi of Ustinov, Gorshkov and Akhromeev in March 1984 set the seal on this enhanced Soviet commitment to India's defence.

The Soviet military contribution today

The Soviet contribution to India's weaponry has been strongest in the navy, less strong in the Indian air force (IAF) and weakest in the army. Things have moved on from the time when two navies, based at Bombay and Visakhapatnam, were respectively Western-equipped and Soviet-equipped and kept entirely separate. Today the navy is composed mainly of Soviet-built vessels: Kashin-2 destroyers, Osa missile boats (both having Styx missiles), F-class submarines, Petia-2 frigates, Nanuchka corvettes, Poluchat large patrol-craft, Natia ocean-minesweepers, and Polnochny landing-craft. Kilo attack submarines are arriving to replace the F-class vessels, and Kresta-II cruisers are to be supplied as well. In February 1988, Moscow leased to the Indian navy, for a four-year term, a nuclear-powered submarine.[35] This is to be armed with conventional weapons and will significantly increase India's potential in the Indian Ocean. At present it is unclear whether this is to be the first of a batch, but it seems likely that it will aid India in building its own nuclear-powered submarine.

Despite the Jaguars and Mirages, Soviet aircraft continue to play the leading role in India's air defence. MiG-21 defence aircraft, MiG-23BM ground-attack aircraft, MiG-25 reconnaissance-interceptors, and MiG-27 fighter-bombers were joined in January 1987 by the first delivery of the MiG-29 interceptors. It seems likely that both MiG-29s and MiG-31s will be produced in India. In April 1988 five updated Tu-142M naval reconnaissance and anti-submarine turbo-props arrived. These long-range, land-based aircraft are able to reach as far as South Africa. The Soviet An-32 is the leading transporter in the IAF. To counteract the feared delivery of AWACS to Pakistan, Moscow offered the Tu-124 Moss, but the Indians refused this and held out for the more sophisticated Il-76. In the army, the principal tanks have been the Indian-built Vijayanta and the Soviet T-54 and T-55. These are all being replaced by T-72 and T-80 tanks, chosen in preference to the British Chieftains and West German Leopards, probably because of pricing considerations. Soviet Mi-24 Hind and Mi-26 Halo helicopters are to be imported. When India failed to buy the American TOW missiles it acquired Soviet AT-6 spiral anti-tank missiles. Its artillery includes a variety of Soviet equipment, especially in the anti-aircraft field.[36]

Pressure from within the Indian armed forces favours diversification of arms imports, but the country's shortage of hard currency continues to place a limit on this. Nevertheless, India is seeking to buy American military equipment in particular fields. General Electric is supplying engines to help it develop light combat aircraft indigenously. The Reagan administration is wary of supplying more sophisticated electronic systems in which India is interested, such as a sea-bed mine-detector and a laser-directed bomb. This is partly because of fears that technology may seep through from India to the Soviet Union. India indignantly denies that this can happen, and takes strong measures to prevent it. The Indian naval base at Visakhapatnam has two separate dockyards, one each for Soviet and Western ships. Soviet personnel are even denied access to some Indian MiG squadrons when the aircraft have been upgraded by the addition of Western equipment.[37] A more important reason why the United States has not supplied the latest military technology to India is the American desire not to upset Pakistan. In April 1988 Frank Carlucci, the US Defense Secretary, visited New Delhi to discuss these issues.[38]

The Soviet Union is also helping the Indian defence sector by buying Indian hardware. This includes avionics for transport aircraft, and the Alouette light helicopter, both produced by Hindustan Aeronautics.[39] Despite its military aid to India, the Soviet Union has not gained any military or naval bases. Its military presence in India is limited to those involved in training Indians in the use and maintenance of new Soviet equipment. In 1986 there were only 200 Soviet military personnel in India. Similarly, the number of Indian military personnel who have received training in the Soviet Union is very small.

The future

Although the absence of *glasnost* surrounding the statistics makes it impossible to draw up a useful balance sheet, it appears that the economic and defence links have benefited both the Soviet Union and India. Arguably, they have benefited India more than the Soviet Union. The USSR apparently saw political advantage in selling oil to India when it was in short supply, and continues to see it in the transfer of state-of-the-art military technology and in the economic and defence relationship as a whole. It is likely that, in so far as resources will allow, India will expand its economic and scientific cooperation with the West at a more rapid pace than with the Soviet Union. This will depend, however, on the willingness of Western countries to share the latest technology, at a price that India can afford. The Soviet-Indian defence relationship, though unlikely to become much closer, will almost certainly continue for as long as the Soviet Union is willing to provide India with arms on a soft-currency basis. There is no sign that Gorbachev sees any reason to stop this, given the regional and global benefits to the Soviet Union of the relationship with India. Equally, India will do nothing to jeopardize the security of its arms relationship with the Soviet Union.

6

SOVIET VIEWS OF INDIA

This chapter seeks to examine how Soviet policy-makers and analysts view contemporary India, explain Indian policy, and justify the relationship between the Soviet Union and a predominantly capitalist state ruled since independence mainly by a single family.

In the absence of direct information, analysts of Soviet affairs have in the past turned to the Soviet specialist academic and policy literature. Since scholarship in the Soviet Union is integrated with ideology and politics, it has been assumed that academic writings reflect the tendencies within the policy-making circles, or alternatively that they represent attempts to influence policy-makers.

The principal academic journals acting as outlets for research on contemporary Indian affairs are *Narody Azii i Afriki*, a specialist journal with a circulation of only about 3,800 copies, published by the USSR Academy of Science's Institute of Oriental Studies and the Institute of Africa, and *Mirovaia ekonomika i mezhdunarodnye otnosheniia* (*MEMO*), with a circulation of 24,000 copies, published by the Academy's Institute of World Economics and International Relations. In a rather different category are the international affairs journals which are intended primarily for foreign consumption and which are published in English as well as Russian: the hard-line *International Affairs*, published by the Ministry of Foreign Affairs and the Znanie [Knowledge] Society; the weekly magazine *New Times*; the glossy *Asia and Africa Today*, published by the Afro-Asian Solidarity Committee together with the Institute of Africa and the IOS; and *Far Eastern Affairs*, published by the Institute of the

Far East. *Narody Azii i Afriki* and *MEMO* carry articles on Indian internal affairs which sometimes make criticisms of Indian policy, while attacking the parties to the right of Congress (I). The IOS publishes a substantial Russian-language annual, *Indiia*.

Richard Remnek, who conducted a major study of Soviet analyses of Indian affairs, reported that in the 1960s there had been a 'growing divergence between the theory and practice of Soviet policy towards India', in which Soviet practical commitments to India were founded on national self-interest rather than on a positive ideological appraisal of the Indian government.[1] Another Western scholar, Stephen Clarkson, in his analysis of Soviet writings from the 1950s to the mid-1970s on development in the Third World, found divergences between the theories themselves. He reported 'unresolved contradictions . . . running throughout the texts'; some writers asserted that capitalist structures and foreign imperialism inhibited development, whereas others favoured capitalist development and encouraged the Third World to accept aid from the imperialists.[2] Analysts were torn between the ideological need to assert the advantages of socialism over capitalism, and the need of the Soviet state to avoid having to support the economies of those countries which might be tempted on to the path of 'socialist orientation'. (This latter category excludes socialist countries such as Outer Mongolia, Cuba and Vietnam, but includes Angola, Ethiopia, Mozambique, Congo, Benin and Nicaragua, and has extended to Algeria, Syria, Libya and Guinea.) Clarkson also concluded, however, that there was a 'growing autonomy of Soviet writings from the ups and downs of Soviet-Third World relations'. This autonomy led him to warn against deducing Soviet policy from Soviet publications, since these represented an actual influence on policy-making rather than being a result of it. There was not yet evidence, however, that academic writings had made a significant impact on Soviet policy towards the Third World.[3]

Changes in Soviet perspectives

From 1917 onwards, Soviet journals carried articles on the tactics to be pursued by the Indian communists, and after independence also debated the nature of the Indian state. The semi-hostile indifference shown by Soviet specialists towards the Congress government in the first years of Indian independence gave way in the mid-1950s, following Khrushchev's visit, to expressions of support for Nehru's foreign policy, which was seen as opposing the exploitation of India by the West. The support extended even to aspects of his domestic policy. Certainly, the view of Modeste Rubinstein in *New Times* in 1956, that Nehru himself was taking the socialist path, was denounced immediately by the CPI and then by leading Soviet scholars. Although Congress was considered to be the party of the national bourgeoisie, Nehru's policy of using the state sector as the motor force of industrial development was seen in some way as laying the basis of socialism in the future. In 1958, Rostislav Ulianovsky argued that 'state capitalism' in India was anti-imperialist in that it strengthened national independence by reducing reliance on foreign firms. The state sector might, however, come merely to serve the needs of capitalism, and it was certainly 'not yet socialism'.[4] Ulianovsky was to play an important role in formulating policy towards India as a deputy head of the International Department from 1966 to 1986. In this position, he would have been conscious of the tensions between the CPI's desire to differentiate its stance from Congress's domestic policy, and Moscow's interest in promoting the stability of a friendly government pursuing a foreign policy which was congruent with that of the Soviet Union.

A further complication in the Soviet analysis of Indian affairs has been caused by the shift in Soviet thinking on the development policies recommended for the less developed countries. Although in 1986 Ulianovsky was still advocating the nationalization of foreign capital, other specialists, from about 1965 onwards, had begun to urge caution over taking steps in the direction of socialist change. Learning the lessons of past mistakes in countries ranging from Ghana to Afghanistan, they have argued against the imitation of the Soviet model of autarky and central planning. The interests of developing countries are best served, they argue, not by industrial development based on import substitution but by playing their full part in the 'international division of labour'. This includes reverting to the production of raw materials for export markets. Further, Soviet economists now encourage Third World countries to maintain a private sector and to cooperate with foreign capital. These views have been advocated since the late 1970s by such notable people as Karen Brutents, a deputy head of the International Department, and Academician Evgeny Primakov, then head of the IOS and now Director of IMEMO and a foreign-policy adviser to

Gorbachev. Brutents stated in 1978 that the Soviet Union was unable to give the LDCs more favourable economic treatment than the West was already providing. In 1980 Primakov, reviewing an IMEMO book which urged LDCs to move quickly to the socialist transformation, argued against this and claimed that Third World countries had been able to make progress within the 'world capitalist economy'. There has been open discussion of the low level of trade between the Soviet Union and the Third World. In the past, such trade was presented in terms of the disinterested aid and equitable treatment given by the Soviet Union to the newly free countries, and was contrasted with the allegedly exploitative nature of the West's links with them. In 1980, however, Oleg Bogomolov, director of the Institute of the Economics of the World Socialist System, stated that the view that relations between the socialist countries and the Third World were based on 'socialist solidarity' was 'erroneous'.[5]

If Soviet policy-makers were to come to share the conversion of the academic specialists towards faith in markets and the private sector in Third World countries, a logical corollary would be to end the favoured treatment of the countries of socialist orientation. Countries pursuing the capitalist path would be entitled to equal treatment. The apparent rise to prominence of Primakov under Gorbachev, the changes in personnel in the Ministry of Foreign Affairs and the International Department, and the emphasis of the new leadership on economic reform in the Soviet Union itself have all contributed to expectations in the West that the Soviet Union is shifting its attention from the countries of socialist orientation to the larger, more influential countries in the Third World which have mixed economies, such as Mexico, Argentina, Brazil and India.[6]

Cooperation with India has for decades been a major element of Soviet policy towards the Third World, but the ideological justification for it has changed significantly. Primakov wrote in early 1987: 'Long gone are the days of far-fetched references to something like India's socialist development, which was interpreted at the time as an important argument in favour of Soviet-Indian cooperation.'[7] It would be wrong to conclude, however, that the Party leadership has abandoned the idea that economic relations between transnational corporations and LDCs are inherently exploitative.[8] In his speech for the seventieth anniversary of the October Revolution, Gorbachev was more at ease in asking questions about the Third World than in answering them. He unequivocally referred to the 'inequitable, exploitative relations' between the imperialist countries and the LDCs.[9]

The domestic politics of India

India today is seen by Soviet analysts not as a purely capitalist society, but rather as a 'multi-structured' (*mnogoukladnoe*) society, in which capitalist relations are penetrating the more traditional sections of the economy. A.E. Granovsky and G.K. Shirokov wrote in a 1986 *MEMO* article of the 'gradual bourgeoisification of the pre-capitalist exploiting strata'.[10] Professor Grigory Kotovsky, head of the Indian and South Asian Department at the IOS, argued in 1984 that the 'affluent groups' that came to power in India with independence used the public sector, state regulation and protectionism to gain control over the economy and to assume the commanding positions formerly occupied by 'foreign monopolies'. The method of 'state capitalism' was used not only to create the state sector but also to produce a fertile soil for Indian-owned private capitalism. The major advances in industrialization were not accompanied by a thorough agrarian reform, since the government's policies in this field were frustrated by the resistance of village landowners and their allies among bureaucrats and politicians. The rapid expansion of the population meant that, in spite of the 'green revolution' and the achievement of self-sufficiency in food, per capita income was hardly increasing at all. According to Kotovsky, the failure of the domestic market to grow in proportion with the capacity of Indian industry forced the government to try to break into the world market. This was the reason behind India's activity in campaigning for the New International Economic Order and also in seeking to develop its economic and political relations with the socialist countries.[11] Granovsky and Shirokov held that India's low growth rates were both a result and a cause of its low participation in the 'international division of labour'. They noted, however, that this in itself protected India, to some extent, from fluctuations in the 'world capitalist economy', and made it easier for the country to follow an independent foreign policy.[12]

Viktor Korneev, in a 1986 monograph, admitted that high hopes had been placed in the 1950s and 1960s on the state sector of the Indian economy as the catalyst of socio-economic change. By the late 1970s, however, the state sector had been subordinated to the private sector, which had responded to the government's policies of Indianization by strengthening its links with foreign capital, thereby defeating the government's ends. A significant number of joint foreign and Indian companies had been formed, which were in fact controlled by foreign capital. During the late 1970s, as a consequence, economic problems worsened, but in the 1980 elections the voters again elected Indira Gandhi Prime Minister, thereby returning to Nehru's path of industrialization.[13] Granovsky and Shirokov noted that the deregulation policies of the early 1980s were, however, leading to the redistribution of income towards the privileged strata. Both they and Kotovsky referred to growing 'social tensions'. The Congress Party, according to Kotovsky, has been pursuing some social policies in favour of the disadvantaged since independence; these have had little success, but have been effective in winning popular support, and thus are 'an important tool in the hands of the ruling classes to maintain social stability'.[14] M.N. Kunshchikov, similarly, asserted in a 1986 article that 'the predominant part of the representatives of the monopolist bourgeoisie' welcomed the re-election of Indira Gandhi in 1980 and of Rajiv Gandhi in 1984. Whereas in a 1981 volume he had spoken of the 'progressive economic measures' introduced by Indira Gandhi, including the nationalization of six large banks, he was now asserting that the monopolist bourgeoisie, after both the 1980 and 1984 elections, had put pressure on the government to adopt a pro-business policy, and that as a result it was promoting 'monopolist processes and state monopoly tendencies'. Veniamin Shurygin reported in August 1987, however, that Rajiv had affirmed more than once that the state sector would be the 'chief instrument' of India's economic development.[15]

Class-consciousness is slow to develop because of the prevalence of traditional religious, caste, communal and ethno-national divisions, which themselves are sustained by illiteracy. Soviet writers on India display particular interest in the caste system and show little optimism that it will be overcome quickly.[16] (This interest reflects a general increase among Soviet scholars in the study of religious tradition in the Third World, which appeared after the Islamic revolution in Iran.) It is important to note, however, that the government has not been accused of promoting intra-communal tensions, which have been blamed on the right-wing parties outside government, and on foreign agencies. The whole Indian bourgeoisie is seen as favouring the preservation of the unified Indian state.[17] The attempts of Rajiv's government to deal with communal conflict in the Punjab and the north-east receive sympathy from Soviet commentators.[18]

It would be wrong to equate academic warnings about social tensions with opposition to the policies which are seen as contributing to it. Following his New Delhi visit, Gorbachev expressed support for the 'realization of plans for progressive transformation ... under the dynamic leadership of Prime Minister Rajiv Gandhi'.[19] During 1987, Rajiv's position came under attack within India, with allegations of corruption linking the Bofors Company of Sweden, among others, to associates of the Prime Minister. As a result there were a number of resignations from the government, including that of the popular Defence (and previously Finance) Minister, V.P. Singh. The Soviet media continued to give backing to Rajiv. His presence in Moscow in July 1987 to open the Festival of India, and his meeting with Gorbachev, received wide publicity in Soviet channels and appeared to give support to his position. Rajiv and his wife, Sonia, were received for dinner at the Gorbachevs' residence – an apparently unprecedented step.[20] Leonid Zhegalov in *New Times* attributed the campaign against Rajiv to 'conflict between the financial and business interests of two rival monopoly groups of private capital'. The United States 'tried to fan' the crisis so as to put pressure on India's foreign policy. Zhegalov implicitly criticized the Communist Parties for initially failing to back Rajiv. 'The left opposition, which at first all but joined in the anti-government chorus, is now distancing itself from the attacks on the INC (I), regarding that party as a guarantee of the preservation of the anti-imperialist orientation of foreign policy.'[21]

A further token of Soviet support for the Prime Minister came in April 1988, when *Pravda* made him the first subject of a series of biographical articles about foreign leaders. Although Shurygin, the article's author, reported that the two communist parties opposed Rajiv Gandhi's social policies, he did not express any sympathy with their criticisms. Even Rajiv's policies to privatize some state enterprises were described without comment. Shurygin gave full approval to the Prime Minister's attempts to prevent secessionism. Noting that members of the Nehru family had been in power for 36 out of the 40 years of Indian independence, he described the family as 'symbols of the national unity of the multi-millioned people', and praised Rajiv's 'wise compromises' in dealing with communal conflict.

Shurygin's article was noteworthy for its praise of the Indian political system. 'Unlike many other "Third World" countries with military and other totalitarian regimes, where coups and counter-coups abound, [India] lives with a full-blooded political life. From the moment of the pronouncement of independence, a parliamentary democracy has been functioning there with all its attributes, such as universal elections, freedom of the press, demonstrations and meetings, and a variety of political parties and other social organizations.' The article concluded by praising Rajiv's 'pragmatic' leadership; he was a 'worthy continuer of the cause of his mother and grandfather'.[22]

Moscow has repeatedly alleged that Pakistan, possibly with the support of circles in the West, has been giving aid to supporters of Khalistan in order to destabilize India. In 1984 Aleksandr Chicherov, head of the International Studies Department of the IOS, accused the Reagan administration of playing a double game in India. It was seeking to improve its relations with India. 'But simultaneously, it is pursuing the policy – which is, of course, carefully concealed – of destabilizing Prime Minister Gandhi's regime, encouraging separatist movements, etc.'[23]

In December 1986 *International Affairs* asserted: 'The Indian authorities' growing concern is also due to the backing which certain quarters in the West, primarily in the United States, Britain and Canada, as well as, most directly, the military administration of Pakistan, give to Sikh extremists and separatists who have emigrated from India and settled down in these countries, something which compels the Gandhi government to insist more and more on stopping terrorism incited from without.' It claimed that the US and British governments were refusing to act against Sikh terrorists operating from their territories.[24] Similar articles appeared regularly in the Soviet press. In August 1987 Tass reported that the Bombay weekly *Blitz* had published a letter from the recently deceased head of the CIA, William Casey, to the head of the right-wing American Heritage Foundation, approving plans 'to remove from the political scene Prime Minister R. Gandhi', to implicate him in charges of corruption and to ignite internal disorders in India.[25] The letter was denounced by the American Embassy as a forgery (and indeed the forgery was so crude that many Indians refused to believe that

Soviet agents could have been involved). It would seem that both Moscow and Rajiv had a common interest in promoting the idea within India that the United States was heaping up trouble for Congress (I).

Indian foreign policy

Western scholars seeking to analyse official thinking in the Soviet Union on Soviet-Indian relations are handicapped by the lack of *glasnost* on the subject that has traditionally prevailed in Moscow, and even, to a lesser extent, in New Delhi. Politicians and officials have shown general reluctance to discuss their differences in public. Under Gorbachev, Soviet officials have generally become more willing to provide information on foreign-policy issues, but as far as Soviet-Indian relations are concerned, there has been, if anything, a closing of ranks between the two governments, except regarding the economic aspects of the relationship.

The extent of Soviet propaganda efforts on behalf of Rajiv provides some idea of the importance that Soviet policy-makers attach to the Soviet-Indian relationship. It is regarded as invaluable not merely for propaganda purposes, but for the real benefits which are perceived as accruing to the Soviet Union. Soviet sources do not, of course, attribute the similarity of Indian and Soviet foreign-policy ends to Soviet pressure on India (or to pressure from South Block on Smolensk Square). They are nevertheless happy to acknowledge the influence of the October Revolution on the Indian freedom struggle, and particularly on Nehru.[26]

An authoritative (if unoriginal) volume, *SSSR i Indiia* ('The USSR and India'), published in 1987 by the IOS, denounced Western bourgeois historians and political scientists for distorting the meaning of the relationship. 'Western political scientists spread slanderous assertions to the effect that the aim of Soviet policy consists in subordinating India to its influence.' On the other hand, suggestions that 'the close cooperation of India with the Soviet Union in some way contradicts the principles of non-alignment' were greatly exaggerated.[27] Chicherov, for his part, had argued earlier that the similarities were due to coincidence of interests. 'The positive thrust of India's foreign policy is reflected in its basically anti-colonial and anti-imperialist stand. This is the main cause of the coincident closeness of many foreign policy moves of India and the

Soviet Union and of profound differences and divergences between the foreign policy of India and the US, although India and the Soviet Union have different approaches to some international problems.'[28] Primakov, in 1987, added another reason for closeness: 'the absence between us of "incompatibilities" in the geopolitical sphere'.[29] Shurygin's *Pravda* article in April 1988 gave full approval to Rajiv's foreign policy, described Soviet-Indian relations as 'unique' and cited the Gandhi-Gorbachev 'Delhi Declaration'.[30]

The volume *SSSR i Indiia* asserted the importance of Soviet-Indian cooperation in keeping the peace in South Asia. While avoiding criticism of the role of India in 1971, it argued that the Soviet government had sought to achieve a solution to the Bangladesh crisis by peaceful means. Emphasizing the importance of the Indo-Soviet friendship treaty, the volume recalled the Soviet help given to India in 1971, but also acknowledged Indian support: 'If the Soviet Union unfailingly helped India to create a healthy political situation in Hindustan (*Indostan*), then India, for its part, actively supported the moves by the Soviet Union to fulfil the Peace Programme adopted by the XXIV Congress of the CPSU in the other regions of our planet.' India had supported Soviet actions aimed at achieving East-West detente, and 'close collaboration' between the two countries had continued 'in the struggle against colonialism and imperialism'.[31] The close relationship had survived the rise of Janata to power, because of India's self-interest; indeed, 'political realities and the needs of the economy showed that the stable basis of Soviet-Indian cooperation is the coincidence of the state interests of the two countries'. A further factor was 'the truly popular character of Soviet-Indian friendship'.[32]

On Afghanistan, the volume quotes Mishra's statement to the UN General Assembly about the Soviet troops having been invited into Afghanistan, as if this were a true reflection of the Indian position. It also reports T.N. Kaul as remarking that 'peace and stability in South Asia depend to a well-known degree on the success of the Afghan revolution'. India was commended for proposing talks between Kabul and Islamabad without prior conditions – a proposal that was acceptable to Afghanistan but not to Pakistan.[33] Finally, by the 1980s Indian and Soviet positions had converged on the freezing of nuclear weapons deployment, on a moratorium on nuclear testing and on the proposals for a nuclear-free and non-violent world enunciated in the Delhi Declaration.[34]

Articles praising Soviet-Indian relations as a model for relations between states of different social systems (and not only in the Third World) appear regularly in the Soviet journals aimed at foreign audiences.[35] Soviet sources emphasize the interest in India and the friendship felt towards it among the Soviet public. The IOS annual on India for 1980 included a bibliography of some 200 books on India published in the Soviet Union between 1970 and 1980.[36] The annual for 1981–2 listed about 250 works by Indian writers which had been translated into Russian between 1975 and 1980.[37]

Soviet analyses of Indian foreign policy emphasize its peace-loving and anti-imperialist nature. Primakov wrote in *Pravda* in January 1987: 'In the political sphere, [India] is already not simply an Asian but also a world great power, whose influence on international events will grow more and more.'[38] Statements such as 'non-alignment is not a policy of neutrality and equidistance', made in 1982 by the Minister of External Affairs, P.V. Narasimha Rao, are cited to show that non-alignment is compatible with support for most Soviet foreign-policy aims and with open criticism of American behaviour.[39] This stance allows Soviet commentators to report without censure Indian interest in buying arms from the countries of Western Europe.[40] Indeed, Soviet publications do not, as a rule, carry any material critical of Indian foreign policy. On the contrary, they tend to be full of praise.[41] Differences are openly acknowledged between Indian and Soviet positions on nuclear proliferation. In 1987 Ambassador Kaul was allowed to express in *Far Eastern Affairs* the Indian view that the NPT was 'discriminatory' in its restrictions on non-nuclear-weapon countries, and had failed in its stated aim of reducing the stocks of nuclear weapons held by those states which were allowed them.[42]

In sum, except in relation to NPT, the Soviet government seems to be prepared to support Indian foreign-policy aims in South Asia, not because it sees India as a surrogate, but because of India's interpretation of non-alignment. Territories where India has dominance are effectively denied to the Americans (and the Chinese and the Pakistanis) and cannot therefore be used as bases for attacking the Soviet Union. This support for India does not extend to the Indian use of force, which might be destabilizing and bring in the Americans or perhaps the Chinese. It has led Soviet diplomats to urge caution in India's dealings with Pakistan and China. Nevertheless, the Indian airlifting of supplies in unarmed aircraft to the

Tamils in Sri Lanka in June 1987, though carried out against the wishes of the Sri Lanka government, won Soviet approval. Moscow presumably expected that the Indian action would not lead to a military response from Sri Lanka or its allies. The Soviet media welcomed the Indian intervention as a 'humanitarian act'.[43] Rajiv's agreement with Jayawardene on the dispatch of Indian troops to the Tamil areas also gained Soviet support as a move against terrorism.

Glasnost does not seem to extend to academics who might wish to advocate changes in the pattern of diplomatic relations in the region or to reassess any aspects of the defence relationship. When the General Secretary says, for example, that the improvement in Sino-Soviet relations will not be at the expense of India, it is impossible to advocate that Soviet interests might be better served by developing relations with China more rapidly. Nevertheless, Soviet policy-makers and analysts still appear to regard the relationship with India as the foundation-stone of their ties with Asia and the rest of the Third World.

7
THE SOVIET PROPAGANDA OFFENSIVE

The Soviet effort
India has been the subject of a major Soviet propaganda offensive, possibly without parallel in any non-communist country since World War II. The resources devoted to publications, press services, radio broadcasts, and cultural centres and festivals indicate a substantial effort to influence Indian public opinion. The Swiss researcher Peter Sager, who published a study of Soviet propaganda in India in 1966, suggested that the cost exceeded $10 million a year.[1] Since then, these activities do not seem to have been reduced. Much of the content of this chapter is based on personal impressions and interviews, including those gained on a visit to India in 1987.

The information department of the Soviet Embassy in New Delhi runs an enterprise known as Soviet Land Publications. This produces a multicoloured illustrated fortnightly journal, *Soviet Land*, published in English and twelve other Indian languages; a weekly journal, *Soviet Review*, in English and eleven other Indian languages; and a children's weekly, *Sputnik Junior*, an illustrated weekly, *Youth Review*, and a fortnightly pictorial review, *Soviet Panorama*, all in Hindi and English. These periodicals are available free of charge.[2] As far as books are concerned, the series 'The World and You' in English, composed of pamphlets by Soviet and Indian writers, is put out by Allied Publishers in New Delhi and is available in Soviet book centres in India at a nominal charge. As in other countries, Soviet books are on sale in India at low prices. Delhi, Bombay, Calcutta and Madras each have several Soviet-run cultural centres and bookstores, some occupying substantial premises. Additionally, the Indo-Soviet Cultural Society (ISCUS), run by Indians and close to the CPI, acts as a channel for Soviet information. The 'Friends of the Soviet Union', established by Indira Gandhi at Sanjay's suggestion in an attempt to take control of some of the Indo-Soviet cultural links, is headed by Congress (I) politicians, currently the former Minister of External Affairs, B.R. Bhagad.

It is not clear whether the USSR is at present giving any direct aid to the funds of the CPI or CPI(M). In Western Europe, communist parties have received indirect help in the form of bulk purchases of their newspapers from libraries in the Soviet bloc. In India, it seems that the Soviet Union gives assistance to a number of newspapers which are not formally linked to the CPI. The most important is the daily newspaper *Patriot*. This takes a pro-Soviet line, but appears to support Congress (I) rather than the CPI. Others include the weekly newspapers *Link*, published by the same company as *Patriot*, and *Blitz*. The CPI central organ *New Age* has its own press service. Peter Sager reports that documents published in *New Age* had been traced back to typewriters belonging to the Soviet Embassy.[3] Today it is openly stated that *Soviet Review* is printed at the New Age Printing Press.[4]

The communist parties

It would be a mistake to seek an indication of the Soviet impact on India's internal affairs in the strength of the communist parties. Although it would probably be an exaggeration to say that the CPI and the CPI(M) are thorns in the flesh of the Soviet-Indian relationship, Moscow has undoubtedly put its greatest efforts into links with Congress (I), and Soviet leaders have tried hard to gain the friendship of Indian prime ministers. The relationships between Khrushchev and Nehru, between Brezhnev and Indira Gandhi (until the invasion of Afghanistan, at least) and between Gorbachev and Rajiv Gandhi have strengthened the links between their two states.

It is appropriate to consider the CPI(M) as well as the CPI in this context, because of the declared support of both parties for Soviet foreign-policy aims, the increased links between the CPI(M) and the CPSU, and the pressures within both parties for merger. The

'Naxalites', the Maoists who split from the CPI(M) in 1968 and continue to have some peasant support, are excluded.[5] The CPI is the larger party, with 479,000 members at the last count, but is getting smaller, while the CPI(M) had 361,500 members and is growing. Some 70% of CPI(M) members are in West Bengal and Kerala.[6] Table 3 shows that the two parties, between them, have consistently won between 7% and 10% of the votes at national general elections. Of the two, the CPI(M) clearly has more support. Its vote in 1984 was concentrated in its areas of traditional strength. Of the 22 seats it won (at a time when Rajiv Gandhi had a landslide victory), 18 were in West Bengal, 2 in Tripura and 1 in Kerala. It was the largest non-regional single party in the Lok Sabha after Congress (I). The CPI vote, by contrast, was more evenly dispersed over the country.

Table 3 Communist performance in Indian General Elections, 1952–84

	1984	1980	1977	1971	1967	1962	1957	1952
Seats won								
CPI	6	11	7	23	23	29	27	16
CPI(M)	22	36	22	25	19	—	—	—
Percentage vote								
CPI	2.7	2.6	2.8	4.7	5.1	9.9	8.9	3.3
CPI(M)	5.8	6.1	4.3	5.1	4.4	—	—	—

Source: T. J. Nossiter, 'Communism in Rajiv Gandhi's India', *Third World Quarterly*, vol. 7 (1985), no. 4, p. 924.

Although neither party has ever formed part of the national government, both have held office in state governments, sometimes in coalition with other parties. The CPI formed its first government in Kerala in 1957, and has been in and out of power since then. The CPI(M) has been in power in West Bengal (an important state with a population of 40 million) since 1977, being re-elected to a third term in 1987. A left-wing coalition led by communists is in power in Kerala. Under the Indian Constitution, these governments have no foreign-policy role. Tom Nossiter suggests that the Soviet Union may have sought to aid the Kerala communists in the 1960s by increasing its imports of agricultural goods from the state.[7] Aid projects have sometimes been located in communist-ruled states, such as the hydrocarbon onshore exploration plan in West Bengal which was agreed at Gorbachev's New Delhi visit. (Congress [I] national governments do ensure, however, that aid also goes to states ruled by their own party.)

Moscow has been encouraging unity between the CPI and CPI(M) since 1965–6, when the International Department realized that the CPI(M) did not hold a pro-Beijing position. A principal obstacle to unity was the question of alliance with Mrs Gandhi's Congress, a policy advocated on occasion by Moscow and supported, with reservations, by the CPI (see Chapter 2). This position was rejected by the CPI(M). In 1979 both parties agreed to form an electoral pact, which meant the end of the CPI-Congress (I) alliance.[8] In the 1980s the two communist parties began to discuss reunification. Achin Vanaik sees the major obstacle to a merger as the 'bureaucratic self-interest of two leadership structures'.[9] Both parties back the principles of Rajiv's foreign policy, but would favour a more anti-American line. Both support Soviet foreign policy initiatives and use language echoing that of Moscow.

At the XIII Congress of the CPI in March 1986, a document was approved which asserted that 'imperialism has stepped up its offensive against the camp of socialism', and stated that against this 'background of the aggravation of the international situation, the Soviet Union and other countries of the Warsaw Pact have launched a peace offensive to rally all the peace-loving forces throughout the world'.[10] The XII CPI(M) Congress resolution in December 1985 had been, if anything, more hard-line. 'The struggle for peace waged by the Warsaw Pact countries, with the support of the people of the world, together with the military preparedness of the Soviet Union which is determined to see that the existing military parity is not upset in favour of imperialism, has so far acted as a strong deterrent against the nuclear warmongers.'[11] The only major difference in foreign policy between the two documents is that the CPI(M) is friendly to China, whereas the CPI is critical of it, especially of its relations with Pakistan. It seems that here the CPI(M) position is closer to that of Moscow, which had already begun to play down its public criticism of Beijing.[12] This is not necessarily a result of Soviet influence; the CPI(M) always maintained a harder anti-imperialist line than the CPI, and also was never as critical of China as the CPI was.

100

Ulianovsky's commentary on the CPI Congress welcomed the expression of 'the idea of the reunification of the communist movement on the principled basis of Marxism-Leninism'. Gorbachev's meetings with the leaders of both parties in New Delhi indicated the importance Moscow continued to attach to unity. Ulianovsky also spoke, however, of the need for 'the unity and cohesion of all truly democratic forces' in the struggle against terrorism and separatism in India. The split in the 'anti-imperialist movement', he said, 'seriously complicates' the struggle.[13] Although he does not make it explicit, Ulianovsky includes the Congress (I) as well as the communist parties in the anti-imperialist movement, and the statement suggests that Moscow would want a reunified communist party to cooperate with Rajiv. This was the sort of policy that led to the CPI setback in 1977. Although Soviet academics claim that the good relationship between the Soviet and Indian governments creates favourable circumstances for the Indian communists, it seems clear that the latter have little to gain from a strategy which reduces them to being effectively the left wing of a Congress-led alliance. Their interests would appear to lie in uniting with Congress (I) against communalist and separatist tendencies, and over foreign-policy questions, but in distancing themselves from Rajiv's domestic economic and social strategy. Experience of the period since 1979 suggests that they will continue to act along these lines rather than in the more pro-Rajiv way that Moscow would apparently prefer.

Public opinion

In short, it does not seem that the possibility of achieving socialism in India, under the leadership of the communists, is seriously entertained by Gorbachev. In any case, the experience of China shows that a communist government is not necessarily a pro-Soviet one. Indeed, much current Soviet thinking on the Third World would support the idea that Rajiv's economic policies of industrialization and modernization by means of both the public and the private sectors represent what is best for India. Rather, the Soviet propaganda offensive in India is aimed primarily at public opinion as a whole, at the Congress (I) and its leaders, at civil servants and diplomats, and at business interests.

India's cultural ties with the West, especially with the English-speaking world, are much greater than those with the Soviet Union or any of the other communist countries. Indian newspapers and journals carry regular analysis of developments in Britain and, to a lesser extent, other Western countries. Books published in the United States and Britain are widely read. Many Indians listen to BBC news every day. British constitutional practices enjoy a high prestige and are still referred to in political disputes. This interest in the West is a natural consequence of British rule and also of the emigration of Indians to other Commonwealth countries and the United States. By contrast, Indians have shown little interest in Russian culture or internal Soviet affairs. The Soviet cultural centres that I visited in Delhi and Bombay were sometimes almost devoid of visitors, although those in Calcutta were better frequented. The only Indian correspondents in Moscow are from the Press Trust of India and *Patriot*. The number of Russian speakers in India is very small, with only about eight universities teaching the language. There are two centres of Soviet studies, at Jawaharlal Nehru University (JNU), New Delhi, and at the University of Bombay.

In spite of all this, the Soviet Union is now held in high esteem in India because of its activity on the world stage and its policies towards India. Such an attitude has not been a constant feature of Indian politics and has varied considerably over the past twenty-five years. The Indian Institute of Public Opinion (IIPO) regularly publishes surveys of Indian attitudes to foreign countries. At present these are based on 1,500 people taken equally at random, after the illiterate have been excluded, from Delhi, Bombay, Calcutta and Madras. In November 1962, after the Soviet Union had taken a pro-China stance in the Sino-Indian conflict, only 1% thought that India should be aligned with the Soviet Union, whereas 36% favoured alignment with America and Britain.[14] This changed rapidly after the Indo-Soviet friendship treaty and the Bangladesh war. In April 1972, only 2% of respondents said that they had a 'very good' opinion of the United States, whereas 43% had a 'very good' opinion of the Soviet Union (an absolute majority of those who had an opinion at all). By August 1977, however, the popularity of the two superpowers was about equal, with the United States even having a slight edge.[15] After the invasion of Afghanistan, the Soviet Union lost ground in the polls until the survey taken in March 1981. This showed a decline in the American position, and the Soviet Union became once more the foreign country regarded most favourably, according to the IIPO weighted average. *The Monthly Public*

Tables 4a–4d A survey of international images, March–April 1986 (in per cent)

Table 4a '*What is your opinion of the following countries?*'

	Very good	Good	Neither good nor bad	Bad	Very bad	Don't know
USSR	32.3	50.6	9.7	1.3	0.9	5.1
USA	18.1	48.3	21.1	5.7	2.5	4.3
UK	8.7	48.7	27.5	4.5	0.7	9.9

Source: IIPO, *Monthly Public Opinion Surveys*, vol. 31 (1986), nos. 8, 9; Blue Supplement, p. iv.

Table 4b '*During the past year or so would you say that relations between India and the Soviet Union (US) have been very good, fairly good, fairly poor, very poor?*'

	Very good	Fairly good	Fairly poor	Very poor	Don't know
USSR	47.1	45.1	2.4	0.4	5.1
USA	8.5	59.3	23.8	2.0	6.4

Source: *Ibid.*, pp. v–vi.

Table 4c '*And in the future, do you think that relations between India and the Soviet Union (US) will improve greatly, improve somewhat, remain about the same, worsen somewhat or worsen greatly under the present Indian government?*'

	Improve greatly	Improve somewhat	Remain about the same	Worsen somewhat	Worsen greatly	Don't know
USSR	28.0	43.3	16.0	1.1	0.2	11.4
USA	10.2	56.1	18.4	3.1	0.5	11.8

Source: *Ibid.*, pp. xix, xviii.

Table 4d '*In your opinion, would it be best for us to strengthen our relations with the Soviet Union (US) in the future, to continue things about as they are, or to lessen our ties with the Soviet Union (US)?*'

	Strengthen ties	Continue about as they are	Lessen ties	Don't know
USSR	58.7	30.0	3.7	7.5
USA	42.5	40.5	8.8	8.1

Source: *Ibid.*, pp. xxiii, xxiv.

Opinion Survey of the IIPO attributed the change to the decision of the Reagan administration to rearm Pakistan as a front-line state. 'The US decision to arm Pakistan with sophisticated weaponry seems to have revived the memories of the Soviet record vis-à-vis India over the last 34 years; the Indian people have come to believe that the Soviet Union would always come to its rescue whenever India faced a crisis.'[16]

From then until 1986, Japan was the most popular country, with the Soviet Union not far behind; but a survey published in 1986, before the Gorbachev visit, put the Soviet Union again in the lead. The survey asked the question, 'What is your opinion of the following countries?' (see Table 4a). The Soviet Union was well ahead of both the United States and the United Kingdom in the 'very good opinion' category. Also of interest were the questions asked about India's foreign relations. *The Monthly Public Opinion Survey* commented that the figure of 92.2% of people saying Indo-Soviet relations were very good or fairly good (see Table 4b) was an 'extraordinary high percentage' (*sic*).[17] Furthermore, 71.3% of interviewees expected an improvement in Indo-Soviet relations (see Table 4c), and 58.7% themselves favoured a strengthening of ties with the Soviet Union (see Table 4d).

Impact on the policy elite
Stephen Clarkson interviewed a hundred policy-makers and academics in 1972 and found that neither in theory nor in practice

have the Soviets had any noticeable impact on the Indian elite's ways of thinking or acting in governmental affairs. Soviet scholarship hardly influenced Indian intellectuals at all, and even the CPI leaders were unenthusiastic about Soviet writings on India.[18] According to P.M. Kamath, India, in its thinking about economic, educational, cultural and scientific affairs, 'heavily leans towards the US'.[19] W.H. Morris-Jones wrote, nevertheless, that 'some part of marxism forms an element in the make-up of most members of the Indian intelligentsia'. He added that this is combined, as in the case of Harold Laski, with a commitment to liberal democracy.[20] Congress thinking is closer to Fabian socialism than to Marxism; ideologists of Congress (I) do not attempt to transpose Marxist class analysis to India.

I conducted interviews with politicians, civil servants, diplomats, business people, academics and journalists in Delhi, Bombay and Calcutta in February-March 1987. This was not a random sample but was biased towards people who had actually had dealings with the Soviet Union. Although there was little support for the Soviet political system or its ideology, the overwhelming majority of those I saw believed that India had benefited from its relationship with the Soviet Union, and that this relationship was likely to continue.[21]

Two exceptions to this prevailing view are Dr B. Vivekanandan of the School of International Studies at JNU, and Bharat Wariavwalla, formerly of the Institute for Defence Studies and Analyses in New Delhi. Vivekanandan saw the invasion of Afghanistan as the latest development in a history of Russian Tsarist and communist expansion, going back 350 years. He referred to 'deep concern in unofficial circles in India' arising from the invasion; for the Soviet action had been justified on the basis of the Soviet-Afghan friendship treaty, and this focused attention on the possible role of the Indo-Soviet friendship treaty.[22] He does not see the Soviet Union as a reliable ally for India. If a conflict broke out with Pakistan or China, the Soviet Union, he points out, would be unlikely to give India military support; after all, it had not given military backing to Vietnam against China in 1979.

In 1985 Wariavwalla, for his part, described the Indo-Soviet relationship as 'stagnant, politically and economically', but added that it could nevertheless last a long time. The Indian government was suppressing 'vital data' on Indo-Soviet economic relations.[23] In an article following the Gorbachev visit, he questioned the Soviet leader's commitment to India. 'Apart from the usual cant on such issues as disarmament, Palestine, apartheid and Central America, which goes into the making of any joint Indo-Soviet declaration, the Soviets and us seem to differ on China, Pakistan and American policies towards the subcontinent. Gorbachev did not make any adverse reference to China and said nothing that would greatly offend Pakistan and the US. Judging from the comment in the Pakistani press, Pakistan seems happy with Gorbachev's sojourn.' He added that South Asia was less important to Moscow now that relations with Washington and Beijing were improving. 'For the past fifteen years, trade between us has not greatly grown nor have the contents significantly changed. Increasing the trade volume by two-and-a-half times as planned now may well remain a paper exercise, as similar ones have in the past.'[24]

These are the views of only a minority. Indeed, the opinion poll evidence, together with my own findings, seems to give grounds to question whether the conclusions reached by Clarkson and others about the low impact of Soviet policy in India are still entirely valid. As far as the business community is concerned, one might expect that Indian exporters who find a soft market in the Soviet Union are keen to protect Soviet-Indian relations, but I have no hard evidence for or against the suggestion that this has had a major influence on Indian policy. (Congress (I) funds, after all, come from people who trade with the West as well.) One can say more categorically that certain parts of the Indian policy and academic elite are very sympathetic to Soviet policy. To an extent not fully appreciated in the West, the Soviet model of development, and in particular the experience of Soviet Central Asia, still demands support in India. Shridhar Shrimali, Reader in Economics at the Bombay Centre of Soviet Studies, pointed out in 1986: 'One can consider an alternative to capitalist development only because of the Leninist interpretation and the successes in the Soviet Union in transforming itself, especially its Asian Republics, [which] has made it possible that today, rather than being a historical successor to capitalism, socialism has become a possible historical substitute.'[25] Vinod Mehta, the Deputy Director of the Indian Council of Social Science Research in New Delhi, wrote in the same year: 'For many of the developing countries which are still fighting to get out of the vicious circle of poverty, the

Central Asian strategy of development or non-capitalist path of development has great relevance.'[26]

One can discount the view that 'whole sections of the Indian administration have been infiltrated by the Soviet services.'[27] What clearly is the case, however, is that influential sections of the Ministry of External Affairs and other senior politicians and civil servants have for some time believed that Indian interests are better served by very close relations with the Soviet Union, regardless of the effect on relations with the USA. The Soviet Union is seen as India's friend against Pakistan and China, and the ally of the oppressed South against the imperialist North.[28] On foreign-policy matters, much of the academic elite is supportive of Soviet foreign policy. Devendra Kaushik, Professor of Soviet Studies at JNU, expressed full support for Gorbachev's Vladivostok proposals, and argued that it was 'time to stop perceiving developments in Asia in terms of superpower rivalry'.[29] He implied that India should take an openly pro-Soviet stance.

Perhaps more important were the views of the practising diplomats. A.K. Damodaran was chargé d'affaires in Moscow at the time of the friendship treaty, and later a member of the Cabinet Secretariat. He remains a supporter of the treaty. The invasion of Afghanistan led him to 'share the worries, unhappinesses and difficulties of most non-aligned countries'. But he noted the 'positive experience of the Soviet Union in the development of our economy, in the defence of our national interests on some critical occasions, and in a continuing interest in the substantial support which we get from that country in our defence industry'. He nevertheless demanded the 'total withdrawal of Soviet troops', and criticized Moscow for 'rationalizing' the 'stumble'.[30] Such views seem common in the Indian elite. Inder Gujral tells how Morarji Desai refused to accept his resignation as ambassador to Moscow in 1977, after the Janata government had been elected on a programme which was critical of Indira Gandhi's relations with the Soviet Union. Desai asked Gujral, 'Why do you think we should have close friendship with the Soviet Union?' Gujral in response asked him to send for notes from the Secretaries for Defence, External Affairs and Commerce. According to Gujral, Desai concluded, on the basis of these notes, that the policy of friendship with the Soviet Union was in the Indian national interest.[31]

A key figure in India's policy towards the Soviet Union, apart from the Prime Minister, who currently also holds the External Affairs portfolio, is the present ambassador to Moscow, T.N. Kaul. He is also a former president of ISCUS. It was he who, as First Secretary, opened the embassy in Moscow in 1947 and later played a major role as Foreign Secretary in formulating the Indo-Soviet friendship treaty.[32] According to G.S. Bhargava, in 1986 Kaul publicly welcomed Gorbachev's proposals for Asian collective security, although they were not approved by Rajiv. Kaul was reported to have ministerial rank and to be senior to both the then Minister of External Affairs, N.D. Tiwari, and Foreign Secretary Venkateswaran, reporting directly to the Prime Minister.[33] In the May 1987 issue of *Far Eastern Affairs*, Kaul again appears to have gone beyond the Indian government position, stating that India 'welcomes the proposals made by Gorbachev at Vladivostok'.[34]

Generally, however, from late 1986 to the present, the government of India has gone out of its way to emphasize its accord with Moscow. N.K. Sharma, General Secretary of Congress (I), deduced from the Gorbachev visit that the 'Indo-Soviet Treaty is very much alive'.[35] Rajiv Gandhi himself has shown none of the inhibitions about the treaty which his mother displayed after 1971. Following his July 1987 Moscow trip, the *Economic and Political Weekly* reported that nobody believed his claim not to have discussed Indian internal affairs with Gorbachev. It was thought that he had retained Soviet support for 'his personal position in the office of the prime minister'.[36]

It would be wrong, however, to deduce from Moscow's level of support for Rajiv that the Indian government was in any sense beholden to the Kremlin. In November 1987 India again abstained at the General Assembly over Afghanistan. Nor should one underestimate the Indian ability to move towards Moscow in order to put pressure on Washington. What is clear is that, despite the weakness of Indian communism, the major part of public opinion and of the foreign policy elite favours maintaining and strengthening the Soviet link, as Rajiv Gandhi has done.

8
CONCLUSIONS

A balance sheet of Soviet-Indian relations

If one examines the whole of the Soviet-Indian relationship from 1971 to the present, it appears that both sides have benefited significantly from their mutual dealings. In the diplomatic and security spheres, each country has gained from the support rendered by the other. This support has not been total or unconditional, but has depended on the perception held by each side of its own interests. In the economic sphere, both sides have profited from the aggregate of the flow of goods, services and aid, and from economic and technological cooperation. It might appear, from the viewpoint of classical economics, that the bilateral trading arrangements lead to an inefficient allocation of resources. Both sides might benefit by reaping the gains of participating fully in the international division of labour and specializing in the production of goods and services where they hold a comparative advantage. In the real world, however, where resources are not always fully employed, barter arrangements provide guaranteed markets for both Soviet and Indian goods which might otherwise be harder to sell, as well as the chance to acquire goods and technology without spending hard currency. Such arrangements are well suited to the traditional Soviet model of command economy, and are appropriate to an economy such as India's, which has a substantial state sector.

What are the principal gains and losses from the relationship for each of the parties? It must be admitted at once that it is difficult to differentiate between the exercise of influence (either Soviet influence on India or vice versa) and the convergence of interests. Thus, what might appear to be Soviet 'gains' from the relationship could well be merely the result of India acting in its own interest. At its most basic, the chief Soviet gain is that India has not entered into a close relationship with either of Moscow's major adversaries, Washington or Beijing. Moreover, it has not seemed likely to do so since the early 1960s. In 1971, Moscow succeeded in its aim of including India in the list of Third World countries with which it has a friendship treaty, using the opportunity provided by the crisis in East Bengal. But, in fact, the position of dominance achieved by India after the 1971 Indo-Pakistani war freed it from dependence on the Soviet Union and allowed it to diversify its relations. The Soviet role in India's victory, however, was very good for Moscow's prestige in India. As regards China, during the period of Sino-Soviet hostility, Moscow's concern that India's efforts to improve relations with China might go too far proved unjustified. Even after the resumption of Sino-Indian diplomatic relations in 1976, the objective difficulties between the two Asian giants prevented any possible return to the friendship of the 1950s. For Moscow, India remained a counterweight to China's power, threatening Beijing with the prospect of fighting on two fronts if it should ever be tempted to war. By 1986, the improvement in Sino-Soviet relations led Moscow to reverse its position and encourage a degree of improvement in Sino-Indian relations.

After the April 1978 revolution in Afghanistan, India's hostility to Pakistan provided Moscow with a potential advantage. At times when the Soviet Union wished to put pressure on Pakistan to prevent it from aiding the Afghan resistance, it could hold out the threat of joint Soviet-Indian pressure on Pakistan on two fronts. However difficult this would have been in practice, given India's jealous preservation of its independence, the threat of such pressure may have been a factor constraining Pakistan's actions in relation to Afghanistan. The role played by India in moving towards a settlement in Afghanistan remains unclear at the time of writing, although the visit of Najibullah to New Delhi in May 1988 was an indication of India's unwillingness to see the Kabul regime collapse.

The Soviet Union has gained from India's support in the NAM, the UN, the Commonwealth and other forums. The refusal of India, the world's largest democracy, to join in Western and Third World criticism of the Soviet invasion of Afghanistan has had great propaganda value for the Soviet Union. Its abstentions in the United Nations voting on Afghanistan probably resulted not from Soviet pressure but from a preference for quiet diplomacy where the Soviet Union is concerned. India made clear its own opposition to the occupation in public and in private, but was not prepared to come into open conflict with Moscow. Similarly, India's recognition of the Heng Samrin regime in Kampuchea, which accorded then with Moscow's policy, seemed not to result from direct Soviet pressure. Rather, it reflected revulsion at the genocidal policy of the former Pol Pot regime, and a desire to show solidarity with Vietnam, which remains in an adversarial relationship with China. Particularly important for Moscow, in its global competition with Washington, is the joint Soviet-Indian 'Delhi Declaration' of November 1986, which seemed to link the government of India more closely than ever before to Soviet positions on nuclear disarmament. Admittedly, the Soviet government had already given support to the earlier 'Delhi Declaration' of January 1985, signed by the leaders of the 'six countries from five continents'. As the 'new political thinking' took hold in the Politburo, there was a certain limited recognition of the influence of Gandhian ideals of non-violence, and in that sense, a convergence of Soviet and Indian perspectives.

In terms of influence on Indian opinion, the Soviet leaders could only have been well pleased at the efforts of Rajiv Gandhi's government to build up the importance of Gorbachev's visit in November 1986 and of Soviet-Indian relations in general. Public opinion remained highly favourable to close relations with the Soviet Union, especially when relations with Pakistan and China were poor. Key foreign-policy advisers, who had observed the relationship for three decades or more, argued in favour of maintaining it. Equally significant for the Soviet Union was the propaganda value outside India of the relationship. Soviet commentators repeatedly hold up Soviet-Indian relations as a model for states with different social systems. India's friendship with the Soviet Union also serves to assure the Soviet population that the peace-loving proposals of the leadership have the support of important peace-loving forces around the world.

What has its involvement with India cost the Soviet Union? Most obvious, perhaps, has been the loss of friendly influence in Pakistan. Despite Soviet wishes, Moscow was unable to carry on playing the

Tashkent game of riding both South Asian horses at the same time. In internal Indian affairs, Soviet backing for Indira Gandhi complicated the task of the Indian communists. The hardest cost to measure is that of the economic and defence relationship. On occasions when Moscow feared a loss of influence in New Delhi – as happened over signs of improving Sino-Indian relations, and after the invasion of Afghanistan – the Politburo made a particular effort to offer Soviet goods to India, evidence that the Soviet leaders were prepared to pay an economic price to maintain their influence. This is not to suggest that the economic exchanges involved were to the overall disadvantage of the Soviet Union, but rather that the terms of exchange were favourable to India. The supply of Soviet oil is one indication of this. Another is the outcome of Ustinov's visits of 1982 and 1984, whereby India was supplied with the latest Soviet defence equipment, including MiG-29s, which must have raised questions in Soviet counter-intelligence about the security of Soviet military technology.

The outstanding gain made by India from its relationship with the Soviet Union remains its victory over Pakistan in 1971, against the opposition of China and the United States. Since then, in spite of India's attempts to diversify its sources of arms, the Soviet defence industry has continued to supply the bulk of India's military imports, as well as helping it to develop its own production. The Soviet Union has acted to counterbalance the arming of Pakistan by China and the United States, and in particular has allayed Indian fears resulting from the American rearmament of Pakistan following the invasion of Afghanistan. Soviet arms have been delivered on terms favourable to India as far as price and credit are concerned, and Moscow has established a reputation as a reliable supplier. By virtue of the friendship treaty, India has succeeded in preventing Soviet arms transfers to Pakistan. Rajiv Gandhi's government has also received Soviet support for its claim that Pakistan has been trying to destabilize it. In the economic sphere, enough has been said already about Indian gains from trade, aid and cooperation with the Soviet Union.

Indian claims to have influenced the thinking of the Soviet leadership on nuclear weapons are difficult to assess. The 'new political thinking' derives from a variety of sources, both Soviet and foreign. Although the Soviet Union (unlike the United States) supported the January 1985 Delhi Declaration and initiated a moratorium on the testing of nuclear weapons, it ended the moratorium when it felt that its vital interests were threatened. What is clear, however, is that India has on the whole maintained its independence and its influential position in the NAM. It has avoided participation in military alliances and the granting of bases to the Soviet Union. It never endorsed Brezhnev's proposals for Asian collective security, seeing them as directed against China. It has likewise avoided support for Gorbachev's Vladivostok suggestion of a conference on security in Asia and the Pacific, concentrating instead on SAARC and bilateral relations with China.

Nevertheless, India has paid a certain price for its Soviet link. Some foreign decision-makers (especially in the United States) have seen the friendship treaty as tying India too closely to the Soviet Union, and have adjusted their view of India accordingly. India was unable to prevent the invasion of Afghanistan; it was, indeed, informed only afterwards. But its reluctance to condemn the Soviet action caused it to lose prestige and influence in the NAM, and was received unfavourably in the West. This, in turn, to some extent limited India's prospects for favourable treatment of its wishes for economic links and arms supplies from Western countries.

On several important issues the two sides have failed to achieve their objectives in relation to the other. The Kremlin was unable to get Indian government backing for its policies on nuclear non-proliferation, and to prevent the 1974 nuclear explosion. It also failed to secure Indian backing for its two major Asian policy initiatives – Brezhnev's proposals for a collective security system, and Gorbachev's ideas for a Helsinki-style conference for Asia and the Pacific. India, for its part, has achieved much, but in the last two years has been unable to obtain public guarantees of Soviet support in any future conflict with its neighbours.

Prospects

In the late 1980s, possible sources of change in the Soviet-Indian relationship are appearing on both the Soviet and the Indian sides. The most important, from the Soviet point of view, is the substantial improvement in Sino-Soviet relations. By the time of Gorbachev's visit to New Delhi, Soviet diplomats were reported to be warning the Indians that Moscow was giving priority to improving relations with Beijing, even though this might be against the wishes of New Delhi.

Western specialists are divided as to the prospects for closer cooperation between the two main communist powers; but it is generally accepted that relations have improved substantially, despite the failure to agree on a summit meeting between Gorbachev and Deng. The principal obstacle seems to be Vietnam's hostile relationship with China, and in particular the continued presence of its troops in Kampuchea. At the same time, it seems likely that both sides have played down the improvement in relations in order to avoid frightening Washington – a factor particularly important in Beijing, where the appetite for American technology is undiminished. There is considerable scope for improving ties between Moscow and Beijing. Nevertheless, the mere fact of the existence of a nation of over one billion people, bordering on the open spaces and forests of Siberia, would give any Russian government reason for caution.

The implication of the Soviet diplomatic warning to India was that the Soviet Union might stay neutral if hostilities flared up on the Sino-Indian border. In principle, the Sino-Soviet relationship would seem much more crucial to Moscow than the Indo-Soviet relationship. At the same time, however, Soviet statements since Gorbachev's Vladivostok speech still sometimes seem to give a higher profile to India. For example, in an interview with the Indonesian newspaper *Merdeka* in July 1987, Gorbachev spoke much more warmly and at greater length of relations with India than of those with China.[1] An *International Affairs* article of October 1987 spoke of 'dynamic progress' in Soviet-Indian relations but only of 'positive changes' in Soviet-Chinese relations.[2] References to Nehru, Indira Gandhi and Rajiv Gandhi and their struggle for peace continue to abound in the Soviet media. It seems unlikely that the Soviet Union would weaken its proven relationship with India for the sake of its less certain relationship with China. Its warnings to India reflect its desire that Sino-Indian relations should improve in parallel with Sino-Soviet relations, so that Moscow would never have to choose in a conflict between China and India. In the event of such a conflict, the Soviet Union would be very reluctant to become involved, but in the final analysis would probably feel obliged to come down on the side of India.

The second possible source of change on the Soviet side is the Soviet decision to withdraw from Afghanistan. The Soviet-Indian relationship has always been sensitive to relations between Moscow and Islamabad. The questions of nuclear proliferation and Pakistan's links with the USA may well remain contentious between the USSR and Pakistan even after the Afghan problem is settled. A significant improvement in Soviet-Pakistani relations would inevitably have some effect on India, but there is little sign of such an improvement at the time of writing. In principle, India welcomes the Soviet withdrawal from Afghanistan, because it should reduce superpower involvement in the region. If American military aid to Pakistan is cut down, Indian anxieties about its neighbour might also be reduced. If, on the other hand, the Afghan war continues, with the resistance receiving backing from Pakistan, then India will continue to turn to the Soviet Union for security support.

The third source of change on the Soviet side is associated with Gorbachev's 'new political thinking' (which, it must be stressed, is not shared by some other senior Politburo members, such as Egor Ligachev). The emphasis on international cooperation for the peaceful settlement of disputes, and on the interdependence of the world, is linked with the improved Sino-Soviet climate and the search for a settlement in Afghanistan. It was apparent in Gorbachev's refusal in November 1986 to promise to come to India's aid in a possible conflict with Pakistan or China. In so far as the new thinking leads to an increase in Soviet participation in international economic organizations such as GATT, interaction and cooperation between Moscow and New Delhi may increase.

The new thinking seems to have other applications in the Third World also. On the one hand, the desire to concentrate resources on the domestic economy so as to make it into a model of socialism, rather than to spend money on the Third World, might lead to a lessening of Moscow's interest in India. On the other hand, it is the countries of 'socialist orientation' which have suffered from this reappraisal, and India seems to be just the sort of country – influential, stable and trying to orient itself to the world market – that the proponents of the new thinking favour. The withdrawal of troops from Afghanistan and the strenuous efforts to promote economic cooperation with India may be symbolic of changes in Soviet policy towards the Third World as a whole.

From the Indian perspective, there are two main possible sources of change. Like the USSR, India has undergone a change of generation in the leadership. Rajiv Gandhi himself appears to be oriented to the West in his tastes and technological interests. Nevertheless, he seems to have taken trouble to assure himself of Moscow's backing. The death of Nehru in 1964 and the defeat of Mrs Gandhi in 1977 did not change the nature of Soviet-Indian relations any more than did the overthrow of Khrushchev in 1964 or the death of Brezhnev in 1982. It is possible, of course, that another leader might be less committed to relations with the Soviet Union.

This potential move towards the West is linked with the second possible source of change – the shifts in the objective needs of India's economy. The country has developed to a level at which Soviet civilian technology is not good enough for its most sophisticated needs, and this would seem to dictate closer economic links with the West and Japan. If the political climate with its neighbours improves, India may feel less need to rely on the support of the Soviet Union. But it would be wrong to expect the expansion of Indian ties with the West to lead to a more pro-Western position in global politics. The West's share of trade with and aid to India is, after all, already considerably larger than the Soviet share.

Proposals have been made to put Soviet-Indian trade on to a multilateral, hard-currency basis, ending the rouble-rupee arrangement. Such proposals would be in line with Rajiv Gandhi's desire to liberalize the Indian economy and with the professed desire of influential Soviet economists to move towards the convertibility of the rouble. The shift to hard-currency trading would, at least in the short run, set back Soviet-Indian economic relations. In addition to the economic disruption, such a shift would have implications for Indian security, since India pays for its Soviet arms imports in soft-currency exports. It is likely that both India and the Soviet Union will want the arrangement to stay in place.

As regards the future of the relationship as a whole, both sides have invested so much in it that they will probably be unwilling to allow any significant deterioration. India could not jeopardize its defence relationship with the Soviet Union, built up over decades. Both Moscow and New Delhi seem to believe that in a changing security environment, the other will be a reliable partner in a crisis. The Soviet Union expects that India will expand its economic links with the West. It is prepared to accept this so long as India does not have to pay a political price for these benefits. At the same time, the

Soviet leadership is going to great lengths to expand its own economic and scientific links with India.

Policy implications
Since India's fear of Pakistan, and to a lesser extent of China, is the principal factor pushing it towards a defence relationship with the Soviet Union, it follows that a reduction in tension between India and Pakistan will be likely to reduce India's reliance on the Soviet Union. If the Soviet Union withdraws fully from Afghanistan, the principal justification for the American rearmament of Pakistan will be removed, and there will be a real possibility of an improvement of Indo-American relations. It seems that the Soviet Union, like the West, will have an interest in reducing tension between India and Pakistan, so that it can maintain good relations with both. In these conditions, a possible outcome might be an attempt by the Western powers and the Soviet Union to mediate between India and Pakistan, and to work out a settlement of contentious issues such as Kashmir. On the other hand, given the failure in the long term of the last attempt at superpower mediation – at Tashkent in 1966 – it might be more profitable to create a climate in which the countries in the region, for example through SAARC, could come to an agreement among themselves. Reconciliation between India and Pakistan will be easier if it is preceded by the restoration of democracy in Pakistan. For India, on the basis of past experience, perceives military regimes in Pakistan as being unstable and more likely to bring about external conflict; thus genuine moves towards democracy in Pakistan should be encouraged.

Such a climate of reconciliation might be facilitated if the main suppliers of arms to India and Pakistan were to restrain sales. In particular, action should be taken to prevent the spread of nuclear weapons in South Asia. This is in the interests of the Soviet Union, the United States and the United Kingdom, and indeed is binding on them as depository states under the Non-Proliferation Treaty. It should be made clear to Pakistan that if it persists in its nuclear weapons programme, serious efforts will be made to curtail the flow of conventional arms to it from the West. The Soviet Union should make equally strong representations to India, to discourage it from developing nuclear weapons.

More generally, Western countries should see it as being in their interests to consider more carefully India's concerns. Western policies which appear to show indifference towards issues which matter to the Third World, such as apartheid (on which Mrs Thatcher in particular is regarded as much too indulgent), will tend to drive non-aligned countries like India closer to Moscow in international politics. As the Brandt Commission pointed out, it is not in the interests of the West for the gap between it and the South to widen. There is scope for the West to expand economic links with India by offering lower prices and better credit terms, and by showing greater willingness to transfer technology. Protectionist measures and regional economic structures which keep out Indian goods should be re-examined. The aim should not be to disrupt links which have developed between the Soviet Union and India, but to explore areas of cooperation between India and the West which are mutually beneficial. With the growing belief in Moscow in global inter-dependence, multilateral projects involving Soviet, Western and Indian participants could be developed to assist the Indian economy.

APPENDICES

A. Indo-Soviet Treaty of Peace, Friendship and Cooperation, New Delhi, 9 August 1971

Desirous of expanding and consolidating the existing relations of sincere friendship between them,

Believing that the further development of friendship and cooperation meets the basic national interests of both the states as well as the interests of lasting peace in Asia and the world,

Determined to promote the consolidation of universal peace and security and to make steadfast efforts for the relaxation of international tensions and the final elimination of the remnants of colonialism,

Upholding their firm faith in the principles of peaceful coexistence and cooperation between states with different political and social systems,

Convinced that in the world today international problems can only be solved by cooperation and not by conflict,

Reaffirming their determination to abide by the purposes and principles of United Nations Charter,

The Republic of India on the one side, and the Union of Soviet Socialist Republics on the other side,

Have decided to conclude the present Treaty, for which purpose the following plenipotentiaries have been appointed:

On behalf of the Republic of India:
Sardar Swaran Singh, Minister of External Affairs
On behalf of the Union of Soviet Socialist Republics:
A.A. Gromyko, Minister of Foreign Affairs
Who, having each presented their credentials, which are found to be in proper form and due order,
Have agreed as follows:

Article I

The High Contracting Parties solemnly declare that enduring peace and friendship shall prevail between the two countries and their peoples. Each Party shall respect the independence, sovereignty and territorial integrity of the other Party and refrain from interfering in the other's internal affairs. The High Contracting Parties shall continue to develop and consolidate the relations of sincere friendship, good neighbourliness and comprehensive cooperation existing between them on the basis of the aforesaid principles as well as those of equality and mutual benefit.

Article II

Guided by the desire to contribute in every possible way to ensure enduring peace and security of their people, the High Contracting Parties declare their determination to continue their efforts to preserve and to strengthen peace in Asia and throughout the world, to halt the arms race and to achieve general and complete disarmament, including both nuclear and conventional, under effective international control.

Article III

Guided by their loyalty to the lofty ideal of equality of all peoples and nations, irrespective of race and creed, the High Contracting Parties condemn colonialism and racialism in all forms and manifestations, and reaffirm their determination to strive for their final and complete elimination.

The High Contracting Parties shall cooperate with other states to achieve these aims and to support the just aspirations of the peoples in their struggle against colonialism and racial domination.

Article IV

The Republic of India respects the peace-loving policy of the Union of Soviet Socialist Republics aimed at strengthening friendship and cooperation with all nations.

The Union of Soviet Socialist Republics respects India's policy of non-alignment and reaffirms that this policy constitutes an important factor in the maintenance of universal peace and international security and in the lessening of tensions in the world.

Article V

Deeply interested in ensuring universal peace and security, attaching great importance to their mutual cooperation in the international field for achieving those aims, the High Contracting Parties will maintain regular contacts with each other on major international problems affecting the interests of both the states by means of meetings and exchanges of views between their leading statesmen, visits by official delegations and special envoys of the two Governments, and through diplomatic channels.

Article VI

Attaching great importance to economic, scientific and technological cooperation between them, the High Contracting Parties will continue to consolidate and expand mutually advantageous and comprehensive cooperation in these fields as well as expand trade, transport and communications between them on the basis of the principles of equality, mutual benefit and most-favoured-nation treatment, subject to the existing agreements and the special arrangements with contiguous countries as specified in the Indo-Soviet Trade Agreement of 26 December 1970.

Article VII

The High Contracting Parties shall promote further development of ties and contacts between them in the fields of science, art, literature, education, public health, press, radio, television, cinema, tourism and sports.

121

Article VIII

In accordance with the traditional friendship established between the two countries, each of the High Contracting Parties solemnly declares that it shall not enter into or participate in any military alliance directed against the other Party.

Each High Contracting Party undertakes to abstain from any aggression against the other Party and to prevent the use of its territory for the commission of any act which might inflict military damage on the other High Contracting Party.

Article IX

Each High Contracting Party undertakes to abstain from providing any assistance to any third party that engages in armed conflict with other Party. In the event of either Party being subjected to an attack or a threat thereof, the High Contracting Parties shall immediately enter into mutual consultations in order to remove any such threat and to take appropriate effective measures to ensure peace and the security of their countries.

Article X

Each High Contracting Party solemnly declares that it shall not enter into any obligation, secret or public, with one or more states, which is incompatible with this Treaty. Each High Contracting Party further declares that no obligation exists, nor shall any obligations be entered into, between itself and any other state or states, which might cause military damage to the other Party.

Article XI

This Treaty is concluded for the duration of twenty years and will be automatically extended for each successive period of five years unless either High Contracting Party declares its desire to terminate it by giving notice to other High Contracting Party twelve months prior to the expiration of the Treaty. The Treaty will be subject to ratification and will come into force on the date of exchange of Instruments of Ratification which will take place in Moscow within one month of the signing of this Treaty.

Article XII

Any difference of interpretation of any Article or Articles of this Treaty which may arise between the High Contracting Parties will be settled bilaterally by peaceful means in a spirit of mutual respect and understanding.

The said plenipotentiaries have signed the present Treaty in Hindi, Russian and English, all texts being equally authentic, and have affixed thereto their seals.

Done in New Delhi on the ninth day of August in the year one thousand nine hundred and seventy-one.

On behalf of the	On behalf of the
Republic of India:	Union of Soviet Socialist
(Sd.) *Swaran Singh*	Republics:
Minister of External	(Sd.) *A.A. Gromyko*
Affairs	Minister of Foreign Affairs

B. Delhi Declaration on Principles for a Nuclear-weapon-free and Non-violent World, 27 November 1986

Today humanity stands at a crucial turning-point in history. Nuclear weapons threaten to annihilate not only all that man has created through the ages, but man himself and even life on earth. In the nuclear age, humanity must evolve a new political thinking, a new concept of the world that would provide credible guarantees for humanity's survival. People want to live in a safer and a more just world. Humanity deserves a better fate than being hostage to nuclear terror and despair. It is necessary to change the existing world situation and to build a nuclear-weapon-free world, free of violence and hatred, fear and suspicion.

The world we have inherited belongs to present and future generations and this demands that primacy be given to universally accepted human values. The right of every nation and every person to life, freedom, peace and the pursuit of happiness must be recognized. The use or threat of use of force must be abandoned. The right of every people to make their own social, political and ideological choices must be respected. Policies that seek to establish domination by some over others must be renounced. The expansion of nuclear arsenals and the development of space weapons undermine the universally accepted conviction that a nuclear war should never be fought and can never be won.

On behalf of the more than one billion men, women and children of our two friendly countries, who account for one-fifth of mankind, we call upon the peoples and leaders of all countries to take urgent action that would lead to a world free of weapons of mass destruction, a world without war.

Conscious of our common responsibility for the destinies of our two nations and of mankind, we hereby set forth the following principles for building a nuclear-weapon-free and non-violent world:

1. Peaceful coexistence must become the universal norm of international relations:

In the nuclear age it is necessary that international relations are restructured so that confrontation is replaced by cooperation, and conflict situations resolved through peaceful means, not through military means.

2. Human life must be recognized as supreme:

It is only man's creative genius that makes progress and development of civilization possible in a peaceful environment.

3. Non-violence should be the basis of community life:

Philosophies and policies based on violence and intimidation, inequality and oppression, and discrimination on the basis of race, religion or colour, are immoral and impermissible. They spread intolerance, destroy man's noble aspirations and negate all human values.

4. Understanding and trust must replace fear and suspicion:

Mistrust, fear and suspicion between nations and peoples distort perceptions of the real world. They engender tensions and, in the final analysis, harm the entire international community.

5. The right of every state to political and economic independence must be recognized and respected:

A new world order must be built to ensure economic justice and equal political security for all nations. An end to the arms race is an essential prerequisite for the establishment of such an order.

6. Resources being spent on armaments must be channelled towards social and economic development:

Only disarmament can release the enormous additional resources needed for combating economic backwardness and poverty.

7. Conditions must be guaranteed for the individual's harmonious development:

All nations must work together to solve urgent humanitarian problems and cooperate in areas of culture, the arts, science, education and medicine for the all-round development of the individual. A world without nuclear weapons and violence would open up vast opportunities for this.

8. Mankind's material and intellectual potential must be used to solve global problems:

Solutions must be found to global problems such as shortage of food, the growth of populations, illiteracy and environmental degradation through the efficient and appropriate uses of the resources of the Earth. The world's oceans, the ocean floor as well as outer space are the common heritage of mankind. A termination of the arms race would create better conditions for this purpose.

9. The 'balance of terror' must give way to comprehensive international security:

The world is one and its security is indivisible. East and West, North and South regardless of social systems, ideologies, religion or race must join together in a common commitment to disarmament and development.

International security can be guaranteed through the adoption of integrated measures in the field of nuclear disarmament using all available and agreed measures of verification, and confidence building; just political settlement of regional conflicts, through peaceful negotiations; and cooperation in the political, economic and humanitarian spheres.

10. A nuclear-weapon-free and non-violent world requires specific and immediate action for disarmament:

It can be achieved through agreements on:
- complete destruction of nuclear arsenals before the end of this century;
- barring of all weapons from outer space, which is the common heritage of mankind;
- banning of all nuclear weapons tests;
- prohibition of the development of new types of weapons of mass destruction;
- banning of chemical weapons and destruction of their stockpiles;
- reducing the levels of conventional arms and armed forces.

Pending the elimination of nuclear weapons, India and the Soviet Union propose that an *International Convention Banning the Use or Threat of Use of Nuclear Weapons* should be concluded immediately. This would constitute a major concrete step towards complete nuclear disarmament.

Building a nuclear-weapon-free and non-violent world requires a revolutionary transformation of outlook and the education of people and nations for peace, mutual respect and tolerance. The propaganda of war, hatred and violence should be forbidden and hostile perceptions with regard to other nations and peoples abandoned.

Wisdom lies in preventing the accumulation and aggravation of global problems which, if not solved today, would require even greater sacrifices tomorrow.

The danger that threatens mankind is grave. But mankind has the power to prevent a catastrophe, and to pave the way to a nuclear-weapon-free civilization. The gathering strength of the Coalition for Peace embracing the efforts of the Nonaligned Movement, the Six-Nation Five-Continent Initiative for Peace and Disarmament, all peace-loving countries, political parties and public organizations gives us reason for hope and optimism. The time for decisive and urgent action is now.

R. Gandhi Prime Minister of the Republic of India	*M. Gorbachev* General Secretary of the CPSU Central Committee

NOTES

For abbreviations, see Bibliography.

Chapter 1

1 Donaldson 1974, 1979; Horn 1982; Robert Litwak, 'The Soviet Union in India's Security Perspective', in George *et al.* 1984, pp. 69–145.
2 Kissinger 1979, p. 868.
3 US Congress, House Foreign Affairs Committee (HFAC) 1985, p. 139.
4 *Foreign Affairs Reports* (New Delhi), vol. 35, nos. 11 and 12 (1986), p. 29.
5 Shearman 1987; Fukuyama 1987.

Chapter 2

1 Kaushik 1971, p. 9. In this chapter I have drawn freely from *ibid.*; Donaldson 1974; Horn 1982; S.N. Singh 1986; Thomas 1986.
2 Cited in S.N. Singh 1986, p. 13.
3 Private information.
4 Sen Gupta 1976, p. 184.
5 Kaul 1982, pp. 255–6; the Soviet source is *SSSR i Indiia* 1987, p. 217.
6 S.N. Singh 1986, pp. 67–82; Horn 1982, pp. 32–43. Horn's speculations about the origin of the treaty are confirmed by Singh and by my own information.
7 Brezhnev 1971, p. 24.
8 The full text of the treaty is at Appendix A.
9 Kissinger 1979, pp. 874, 886.

10 Donaldson 1974, pp. 225–37; Horn 1982, pp. 66–71; Kissinger 1979, pp. 886, 913; S.N. Singh 1986, pp. 94–6; Sen Budraj 1973a, pp. 482–95.

11 Cited in Donaldson 1979, p. 46.

12 Horn 1982, pp. 85–93; S.N. Singh 1986, pp. 101–2; Sen Gupta 1976, pp. 150–4, 194 (*Pravda* quotation).

13 The speeches are excerpted in *India and the Soviet Union* 1975, pp. xxxiii–xxxxv (quotations pp. xxxvi, xxxix, xxxxii, xxxviii).

14 Brezhnev 1976, pp. 18–19.

15 S.N. Singh 1986, p. 135.

16 *The Statesman*, 27 April 1977, cited in Horn 1982, p. 149.

17 Gujral 1986, pp. 157–65.

18 *Vizit* 1977, p. 29.

19 Sen Gupta 1981, p. 37.

20 Brezhnev 1981, p. 18.

21 Tariq Ali, pp. 271–2; Horn 1983a, p. 257.

22 Horn 1983a, pp. 258–9; US Congress HFAC 1985, p. 132; Ulianovsky 1983; Thornton 1983, pp. 20–1.

23 'Rech' General'nogo sekretaria TsK KPSS Iu. V. Andropova', *Pravda*, 23 November 1982.

24 'Inde', *Le Monde*, 5 April 1983; 'Andropov May Visit India Next Winter', *The Hindu*, 17 April 1983.

25 Mary Anne Weaver, 'Sharma's Shame', *Sunday Times*, 2 October 1983; Kuldip Nayar, 'Moscow Swings behind Mrs Gandhi', *The Times*, 27 September 1983.

26 The previous paragraphs draw on Hayat 1984, pp. 60–5; Litwak, in George *et al.*, p. 133; Kaushik 1985, p. 8; S.N. Singh 1986, pp. 207–19; Bhabhani Sen Gupta, 'For Better or for Worse', *IT*, 31 March 1984, pp. 43–4; Zagoria 1985, pp. 30–2.

27 Cohen 1985, p. 24; S.N. Singh 1986, p. 244.

28 Kaushik 1985, p. 9.

29 *Ibid.*, pp. 8–9.

30 Georgiev 1985a, pp. 42–3, 46 (quotation).

31 Rubinstein 1986, p. 358.

32 Zagoria 1986, pp. 24–6; Gujral 1986, pp. 158–60; Akhter 1986, p. 89.

33 Kreisberg 1986, p. 12; IMF, *Directory 1986*, p. 534.

34 Narain 1986, p. 267.

35 Associated Press, 11 October 1985, in Bohdan Nahaylo, 'Gorbachev's Asian Debut: The Visit to India', *Radio Liberty Research Bulletin* (*RLRB*), RL 440/86, 21 November 1986, p. 3.

36 'Vstrecha M.S. Gorbacheva s R. Gandi', *Pravda*, 27 October 1985 (quotation). For a Western account, see John Elliott, 'Gandhi Rejects Pakistan Denials', *The Financial Times*, 28 October 1985.

37 Andrei A. Gromyko, 'Velikaia doch' Indii', *Pravda*, 29 October 1985.
38 'The USSR This Week', *RLRB*, RL 393/85, 22 November 1985, p. 9.
39 *BBC Summary of World Broadcasts (SWB)*, *SWB*/FE/W1371/A/31, 8 January 1986.
40 Gorbachev 1986, p. 82.
41 'Rubezhi sotrudnichestva', *Pravda*, 1 May 1986.
42 'Beseda M.S. Gorbacheva s P. Shiv Shankarom', *Pravda*, 15 June 1986.
43 A. Filippov, 'Vopreki natsional'nym interesam', *Pravda*, 22 July 1986.
44 'Nauka mirnoi zhizni', *Pravda*, 24 November 1986.
45 *Indo-Soviet Friendship* 1986, pp. 48–52.
46 'Rech' M.S. Gorbacheva', *Pravda*, 28 November 1986; 'Sovmestnaia press-konferentsiia M.S. Gorbacheva i R. Gandi', *Pravda*, 29 November 1986.
47 'Sovmestnaia' (see n. 46), and John Elliott, 'Soviet Union and India Plan Joint Ventures', *The Financial Times*, 28 November 1986.
48 Marguerite Johnson, 'Cordial Passage to India', *Time*, 8 December 1986.
49 'Sovmestnoe sovetsko-indiiskoe zaiavlenie', *Pravda*, 28 November 1986.
50 Eric Silver, 'Gandhi Says Pakistan was Involved in Murder Plot', *Guardian*, 10 October 1986.
51 'Rech' tovarishcha Gorbacheva M.S.', *Pravda*, 29 July 1986.
52 *Indo-Soviet Friendship* 1986, p. 8.
53 Bhabhani Sen Gupta, 'A Different Beginning', *IT*, 15 December 1986, p. 54.
54 'Sovmestnaia' (see n. 46).
55 'Vysokaia stepen' vzaimodeistviia i doveriia. Vystuplenie M.S. Gorbacheva', *Pravda*, 28 November 1986.
56 S. Venkatesh, 'Soviet Pledge to Guard India's Interests', *The Statesman*, 28 November 1986.
57 'Sovmestnaia' (see n. 46).
58 This irony was drawn to my attention by Professor R.V.R. Chandrasekhara Rao of the University of Hyderabad.
59 The full text of the declaration is at Appendix B.
60 'Sovmestnoe' (see n. 49).
61 'The Second Honeymoon', *IT*, 15 December 1986, p. 44.
62 'India, USSR Want N-Arms Destroyed by End of Century', *Hindustan Times*, 28 November 1986.
63 'Besedy M.S. Gorbacheva s General'nym sekretarem Natsional'nogo soveta KPI R. Rao i General'nym sekretarem TsK KPI(M) E. Nambudiripadom', *Pravda*, 28 November 1986; 'Fraternal Status on CPI-M Conferred', *Hindustan Times*, 28 November 1986.

129

64 *Pravda* , 3, 4 and 5 July 1987, and 25, 26 and 27 November 1987;
'L'Inde et l'URSS signent un vaste accord de cooperation scienti-
fique', *Le Monde*, 5–6 July 1987; Derek Brown, 'Gandhi Profits from
Moscow Visit', *Guardian*, 6 July 1987; Michael Hamlyn, 'Soviet Glit-
ter to Woo India as Gandhi Warms to US', *The Times*, 24 November
1987; K.K. Sharma, 'Soviet Credits for India', *The Financial Times*,
25 November 1987.

Chapter 3

1 Premdev 1985, pp. 31–2.
2 Shahi 1987, p. 4.
3 Mansingh 1984, p. 40.
4 *Ibid.* , p. 41.
5 IISS 1987a, p. 156.
6 Thomas 1986, p. 184 and *SIPRI Yearbook 1987*, p. 174.
7 *SIPRI Yearbook 1987*, p. 139.
8 'Defence Spending up 22%', *Times of India* (New Delhi), 1 March
 1987. The 22% referred to the increase over the revised estimates for
 1986–7, which themselves were substantially higher than the original
 estimates.
9 See Shahram Chubin, 'The Place of India in US Foreign Policy', in
 George *et al.*, pp. 197–9.
10 Rosemary Foot, 'The Sino-Soviet Complex and South Asia', in *South
 Asian Insecurity and the Great Powers*, p. 192. Rosemary Foot, referring to the 1960s, wrote, 'New Delhi was of paramount importance to
 Moscow as a counterweight to Beijing.'
11 Cohen 1985, pp. 21–2.
12 *Ibid.*, p. 22. Compare also Horn 1983b.
13 Foot, in *South Asian Insecurity*, p. 196.
14 Thornton 1987, p. 461.
15 Mukerjee 1986, p. 109.
16 Horn 1982, p. 181.
17 *Indian Express*, 3 January 1980, cited in Ahmad 1983, p. 79.
18 Prasad 1980, p. 636; Ghosh and Panda 1983, pp. 261–2.
19 S.N. Singh 1986, p. 289, n. 41.
20 Dutt 1984, p. 373; Ghosh and Panda 1983, pp. 261–2.
21 *Los Angeles Times*, 17 January 1980, cited in Horn 1982, p. 183.
22 Prasad 1980, p. 637.
23 *Ibid.*, p. 638.
24 *Ibid.*, p. 637.
25 Ahmad 1983, pp. 81–2.
26 Litwak, in George *et al.*, 1984, pp. 112–13; Robinson 1981, p. 26.
27 Prasad 1980, p. 638.

28 Robinson 1982, pp. 25–6; S.N. Singh 1986, p. 182; Kaushik 1985, pp. 6–7, 15; Horn 1983a, pp. 255–6 (including final quotation from *Overseas Hindustan Times*, 8 January 1982).

29 Griffith 1982, p. 40.

30 See Agha Shahi, 'Pakistan's Relationship with the United States', in *Soviet-American Relations* 1987, pp. 163–81.

31 Lifschultz 1986, pp. 71–7. A summary of this article was published in *The Muslim*, causing a stir in Pakistan. See Babar Ali, 'Pakistani-US Military Relationship in the 1980s' *EPW*, 4 April 1987, pp. 588–90.

32 Mikhin 1986; Georgiev 1986; Kovalenko 1986, pp. 20–1.

33 *Pravda* , 8 May 1987.

34 *The Financial Times*, 9 May 1987.

35 IISS 1987b, p. 140.

36 *SIPRI Yearbook 1987*, pp. 140–1.

37 Tellis 1986, p. 46.

38 *SIPRI Yearbook 1987*, p. 207.

39 Kuldip Nayar, 'We Have the A-Bomb, Says Pakistan's "Dr Strangelove"', *Observer* (London), 1 March 1987.

40 Christopher Thomas, 'Reagan Seeks Legal Loophole for Pakistan Aid Programme', *The Times*, 10 March 1987.

41 Mikhin 1986, p. 87.

42 'Pak-US Relations', *Pakistan Times* (Islamabad), 4 February 1988; also Hyman 1986.

43 Eric Silver, 'Gandhi Says Pakistan was Involved in Murder Plot', *Guardian*, 10 October 1986.

44 See various reports in *IT*, 28 February 1987.

45 'Fresh Pak Attack on Siachin Repulsed', *National Herald* International Edition (New Delhi), 15–21 January 1988.

46 Amalendu Das Gupta, 'Pressures on Security', *The Statesman*, 21 February 1987.

47 Zahur Ul Haq, 'India's War Fever', *Pakistan Times*, 1 February 1987.

48 V. Skosyrev, 'Kogda trony shataiutsia', *Izvestiia*, 21 August 1986; Vsevolod Ovchinnikov, 'Kommivoiazher fabrikantov smerti', *Pravda*, 21 October 1986; Pleshov 1987.

49 See Iu. Shtykanov, 'Karateli protiv pushtunov', *Izvestiia*, 6 August 1987; Husain Haqgani, 'The Unseen Soviet Hand', *FEER*, 29 October 1987.

50 Inder Malhotra, 'Seminar Report', in *Security without Nuclear Weapons* 1986, p. 209.

51 Cohen 1985, pp. 26–31.

52 Abdul Majid Khan, 'Pak-USSR Economic Relations', *Pakistan and Gulf Economist* (Karachi), 8–14 November 1986, pp. 37–8.

53 Ali 1983; Kadeer 1985; Popatia 1985.

54 Ali 1983, pp. 1021–32.
55 Shahi 1987, p. 5.
56 'Geneva Talks – Decision Deferred', *Dawn*, 13 March 1987. See also Ghazi Salahuddin, 'Things Fall Apart', *Dawn*, 12 March 1987; M.B. Naqvi, 'Russian Moves: What Should Be Our Response?' *Dawn*, 28 February 1987.
57 Shahi 1987, pp. 10–11.
58 *Pravda*, 7 October 1987, p. 5.
59 Kovalenko 1986, p. 26.
60 'Rech' tovarishcha Gorbacheva M.S.', *Pravda*, 29 July 1986.
61 *Pravda*, 9 and 11 September 1986.
62 *Pravda*, 24 February 1987.
63 Jetly 1986; G.S. Misra, 'Sino-Soviet Dialogue', in *Yearbook on Indian Foreign Policy 1984–85*, pp. 147–54.
64 Malhotra, in *Security without Nuclear Weapons* 1986, pp. 201–9.
65 Ajoy Bose, 'Chinese Sharply Attack India's "Illegal Seizure" of Border State', *Guardian*, 13 December 1986; Shekhar Gupta with Indranil Banerjie, 'Face to Face', *IT*, 31 December 1986, pp. 74–5.
66 Dilip Bobb, 'Escalating Tension', *IT*, 15 May 1987, pp. 52–3; Jonathan Mirsky, 'Chinese Troops Wounded in Clash with India', *Observer*, 7 June 1987.
67 'Over the Week', *National Herald* International Edition (New Delhi), 15–21 January 1988.
68 K. Subrahmanyam, 'Pak Nuclear Programme', *Times of India* (New Delhi), 28 February 1988.
69 '"Pakistani Bomb" Threat Forces Indian Policy Review', *Guardian*, 28 April 1987.
70 Thomas 1986, p. 47. See also Rizvi 1987, pp. 131–5.
71 Potter 1985, pp. 474–7.
72 Benevolensky 1986, p. 237.
73 For example, Vladilen Baikov, 'Opasnoe partnerstvo', *Pravda*, 12 March 1987; Iu. Gavrilov, 'Popustitel'stvo Vashingtona iadernym ambitsiiam Islamabada', *Sovetskaia Rossiia*, 13 March 1987; Leonid Zhegalov, 'A Screwdriver for Islamabad', *NT*, 27 April 1987, No. 16, pp. 22–3; V. Soldatov, 'Vokrug "islamskoi bomby"', *Izvestiia*, 28 April 1987.
74 Benevolensky 1986, p. 237.
75 On SAARC, see Pran Chopra, 'The Rising Salience of Politics in SAARC', in *Yearbook on India's Foreign Policy, 1984–85*, pp. 91–103.
76 Veniamin Shurygin, 'V interesakh dobrososedstva', *Pravda*, 12 December 1985; Kunshchikov 1986b.
77 Leonid Zhegalov, 'A Humanitarian Act', *NT*, 22 June 1987, no. 24, pp. 7–8.

78 *SWB* SU/8636/A3/10–11 (3 August 1987); 'Novyi etap otnoshenii',
 Pravda, 3 August 1987; N. Paklin, 'Zhertvy nasiliia', *Izvestiia*, 10
 October 1987; Sergei Irodov, 'Abiding by the Agreement', *NT*, 1988,
 no. 6 (February), p. 21.
79 Horn 1987, p. 698.

Chapter 4
1 Rais 1986, p. 161.
2 Rais 1986, pp. 159–61; Donaldson 1979, pp. 34–6; Litwak in George
 et al., pp. 126–9.
3 J. Singh 1985, p. 473.
4 Kohli 1986, p. 159.
5 *Pravda* , 28–29 November 1986; Kovalenko 1987, pp. 28–9.
6 *Soviet News* , 14 October 1987, p. 365.
7 Rajan 1985, pp. 53–77; US Congress HFAC 1985, pp. 137–8.
8 Re-translated from V.L. Kushpel and A.I. Fialkovsky, 'Indiia-pred-
 sedatel' dvizheniia neprisoedineniia (1983–1986)', in *Indiia 1985–86*, p.
 182.
9 US Congress HFAC 1985, p. 126.
10 Jayashekar, 'Indo-Soviet Relations: Continuing Relevance', *Yearbook
 on India's Foreign Policy 1984–85*, p. 179.
11 Benevolensky 1986, p. 229.
12 'Rech' tovarishcha Gorbacheva M.S.', *Pravda*, 29 July 1986.
13 T.N. Ninan, 'India's Healing Touch', *IT*, 30 September 1986, p. 27;
 Narain and Dutta 1987, p. 191; Zimbabwe 1987.
14 K.D. Kapur 1983, p. 190.
15 Kushpel and Fialkovsky, pp. 181–4, 192 (see n. 8).
16 Six Nation Summit, pp. 13–14.
17 *Soviet News* , 5 November 1986, p. 461; Kovalenko 1987, pp. 24–5;
 Alimov 1986; Sergiev 1986.
18 See Tomilin 1987; M.S. Gorbachev, 'O khode realizatsii reshenii
 XXVII s''ezda KPSS i zadachakh po uglubleniiu perestroiki', *Pravda*,
 29 June 1988.
19 H. Kapur 1987, p. 578.
20 Roger E. Kanet, 'Commentary', in US Congress, Joint Economic
 Committee 1987, vol. 2, p. 544.
21 Rose 1986, p. 100.
22 'The Odd Country Out', *The Hindu*, 20 October 1987.
23 Chadda 1986, p. 1132.
24 S.N. Singh 1983; Chadda 1986.
25 Wirsing 1985, pp. 273–83.

26 The theme of Indo-US relations cannot be pursued here. See also Frankel 1986; Harrison 1986; Travis 1986; Chubin, in George *et al.*, pp. 147–234; Leonidov 1986.

Chapter 5

1 Glebov 1988, p. 30.
2 Premdev 1985, pp. 166–7.
3 Stanislaus 1975, p. 167.
4 Horn 1982, p. 128.
5 *Ibid.*, pp. 138–9.
6 OECD 1986, pp. 81–2.
7 CIA 1980, p. 108; 1985, p. 110; 1986, p. 112.
8 UN 1985, p. 358.
9 See *Statistical Outline of India 1986–87*, p. 148.
10 According to the Indian Ministry of Planning, Central Statistical Office (CSO), *Statistical Abstract India 1984*, pp. 270–2.
11 For example, India CSO, *Basic Statistics 1985*, pp. 116–17.
12 As in India CSO, *Statistical Abstract 1984*, pp. 269–271 and *Statistical Pocket Book India 1984*, p. 133.
13 Bach 1987, p. xiii.
14 India CSO, *Basic Statistics 1985*, pp. 116–17.
15 The dollar figures provided in the IMF *Direction of Trade Statistics* are based on extrapolations from 1982 onwards, and I have therefore preferred to use the data provided directly by the Soviet and Indian ministries.
16 Calculated by the author from successive volumes of the annual *Vneshniaia torgovlia SSSR. Statisticheskii obzor*.
17 India CSO, *Statistical Pocket Book India 1985*.
18 Santosh Mehrotra, 'The Political Economy of Indo-Soviet Relations', in *Soviet Interests in the Third World* 1985, pp. 229–30.
19 Mukerjee 1987, p. 24; 'Indo-Soviet Economic Relations' 1986, p. 25.
20 'Indo-Soviet Economic Relations' 1986, p. 25.
21 *Indo-Soviet Friendship* 1986, pp. 34–8; John Elliott, 'Soviet Union and India Plan Joint Ventures', *The Financial Times*, 28 November 1986; 'Sovmestnoe sovetsko-indiiskoe zaiavlenie', *Pravda*, 28 November 1986.
22 *FEER*, 5 February 1987, pp. 50–5.
23 Alekseev 1987, p. 49.
24 V. Korovikov, 'Kachestvenno novyi etap', *Pravda*, 30 March 1987.
25 Segon 1987, p. 9.
26 Inder Malhotra, 'Rajiv-Ryzhkov Talks Tighten Friendship Bonds', *India Abroad*, 25 December 1987.

27 Surajeet Das Gupta, 'A Rush for Russia', *IT*, 15 January 1988, pp. 76–7.
28 Lincoln Kaye, 'Moscow's Indian Summer', *FEER*, 5 February 1987, p. 51.
29 US Arms Control and Disarmament Agency 1987, p. 146. CIA estimates are based on the dollar costs which would be incurred in producing equipment in the USA – and may be completely unrelated to the price charged by the Soviet Union.
30 Mohamedi 1987, p. 9.
31 Kramer 1987, pp. 58–63.
32 Hayat 1984, p. 53; Akhter 1986, p. 99; S.N. Singh 1984, pp. 711–12. The latter is a useful source on the Soviet-Indian arms relationship.
33 Akhter 1986, p. 101.
34 S.N. Singh 1984, pp. 707–9; Akhter 1986, p. 100; Hayat 1984, pp. 58–63; Thornton 1984, pp. 13–14; US Congress HFAC 1985, pp. 130–2; Banerjee 1987, p. 3.
35 'India Inducts N.Sub Into Navy', *Pakistan Times*, 4 February 1988.
36 The previous paragraphs are mainly based on Thomas 1986, pp. 162–74; Banerjee 1987, pp. 3–5.
37 Mukerjee 1986, p. 118.
38 Michael Hamlyn, 'Carlucci Handed Indian Arms List', *The Times*, 5 April 1988.
39 Mohamedi 1987, p. 6.

Chapter 6

1 Remnek 1975, p. 49.
2 Clarkson 1979, pp. 249–50.
3 *Ibid.*, p. 260.
4 Donaldson 1974, pp. 138–41 (quotation p. 141); cf. Hough 1986, pp. 112–13, 117–19. Changing Soviet perspectives on India are discussed in Sahai-Achuthan 1983.
5 Ulianovsky 1986a; Remnek 1975, pp. 241–50; Zamostny 1984, p. 223–35; Valkenier 1986.
6 Litwak and MacFarlane 1987, p. 32.
7 Evgeny M. Primakov, 'Krupnyi shag vpered. Razmyshleniia posle vizita M.S. Gorbacheva v Indiiu', *Pravda*, 5 January 1987.
8 See Bellis 1987, p. 43.
9 *Pravda* , 3 November 1987.
10 Granovsky and Shirokov 1986, p. 66.
11 Kotovsky 1984, pp. 1131–7.
12 Granovsky and Shirokov 1986, p. 68.

13 Korneev 1986, pp. 13–14, 17.
14 Granovsky and Shirokov 1986, pp. 67, 73–5; Kotovsky 1984, pp. 1137–9.
15 Kunshchikov 1986a, pp. 82–6 and 1981, p. 180; Shurygin 1987, p. 19.
16 Kotovsky 1984, p. 140; Iurlova 1986; Gendin 1986.
17 Granovsky and Shirokov 1986, p. 67.
18 Belsky *et al.* 1987; Valentin Korovikov, 'Separatisty nakaliaiut obstanovku', in *Pravda*, 1 August 1986; Leonid Zhegalov, 'Punjab Again', *NT*, 1 June 1987, pp. 7–8; Riabinin 1986, pp. 119–24.
19 'Otvet M.S. Gorbacheva na pis'ma i privetstviia indiiskikh grazhdan', *Pravda*, 13 December 1986.
20 *Pravda*, 2–5 July 1987; Derek Brown, 'Gandhi Profits from Moscow Visit', *Guardian*, 6 July 1987.
21 Leonid Zhegalov, 'Attacks from within, Pressure from without', *NT*, 25 May 1987, pp. 11–13; *idem*, 'Under Pressure', *NT*, 15 June 1987, pp. 12–13.
22 Veniamin Shurygin, 'Radzhiv Gandi', *Pravda*, 8 April 1988.
23 Chicherov 1984, pp. 1126–7.
24 Riabinin 1986, p. 123.
25 'Bezporiadki v Indii i TsRU', *Pravda*, 2 August 1987.
26 Komorov 1987, pp. 6–9. For an earlier discussion of the content of Soviet propaganda aimed at India, see Hensel 1985, pp. 240–5.
27 *SSSR i Indiia* 1987, p. 12.
28 Chicherov 1984, p. 1126.
29 Primakov (see n. 7).
30 Veniamin Shurygin, 'Radzhiv Gandi', *Pravda*, 8 April 1988.
31 *SSSR i Indiia* 1987, pp. 222–34 (quotation on p. 231).
32 *Ibid.*, p. 238.
33 *Ibid.*, pp. 239–40 (quotation on p. 240).
34 *Ibid.*, pp. 242–8.
35 For example, Rumiantsev 1984; Georgiev 1985b; Vavilov 1986; Georgiev 1987; Losev 1987; Alekseev 1987. The most recent *MEMO* article dedicated to Soviet-Indian friendship, however, appears to be Garev and Tsaplin 1981.
36 *Indiia 1980. Ezhegodnik*, pp. 330–4.
37 *Indiia 1981–1982. Ezhegodnik*, pp. 301–10.
38 Primakov (see n. 7).
39 S.V. Velichkin, 'Vneshniaia politika Indii', in *Indiia 1983. Ezhegodnik*, p. 276.
40 *Ibid.*, pp. 272–3.
41 Georgiev 1984; Velichkin (see n. 39) pp. 252–76; Iurlov 1987, p. 119.
42 Kaúl 1987, p. 17.
43 Leonid Zhegalov, 'A Humanitarian Act', *NT*, 22 June 1987; also N. Paklin, 'Za politicheskii dialog', *Izvestiia*, 7 June 1987.

Chapter 7

1 Sager 1966, p. 9.
2 'Books from USSR', *Soviet Review* (New Delhi), 12 February 1987, pp. 57–8.
3 Sager 1966, pp. 167, 201–7.
4 *Soviet Review* , 12 February 1987, p. 1.
5 On the origins of the split in the Indian communist movement, see Donaldson 1974, Sen Gupta 1972, Ram 1969, and Nossiter 1982.
6 Staar 1987, p. 46.
7 Nossiter 1982, pp. 56–7.
8 *Ibid.*, pp. 201–2, 259.
9 Vanaik 1986, p. 61.
10 Communist Party of India (CPI) 1986, p. 71.
11 Communist Party of India (Marxist) (CPI[M]) 1985, p. 8.
12 Compare CPI 1986, pp. 70–80, with CPI(M) 1985, p. 8.
13 Ulianovsky 1986b, p. 53.
14 Donaldson 1974, p. 163.
15 Donaldson 1979, pp. 23–5.
16 *Monthly Public Opinion Survey* 1981, pp. ii-iii.
17 *Monthly Public Opinion Survey* 1986, p. i.
18 Clarkson 1973, pp. 715–24.
19 Kamath 1984, p. 273.
20 Morris-Jones 1971, p. 253.
21 Howard Hensel reported similar findings after interviews in 1984. See Hensel 1985, pp. 245–8.
22 Vivekanandan 1980, pp. 63, 72–5.
23 Wariavwalla 1985, pp. 310–13.
24 Wariavwalla 1987, p. 39.
25 Shrimali 1986, p. 1.
26 Mehta 1986, p. 51.
27 Domenach 1985, p. 145.
28 The cross-party consensual nature of this view is argued in Ghosh and Panda 1983.
29 Devendra Kaushik, 'Convergence of Approaches', in *Reykjavik Summit* 1986, pp. 22–4.
30 Damodaran 1980, pp. 589, 591, 595.
31 Inder K. Gujral, 'Summit and Peace in Asia', in *Reykjavik Summit* 1986, p. 55.
32 T.N. Kaul, 'Kak ia narushil diplomaticheskuiu traditsiiu', *Literaturnaia gazeta*, 15 March 1987; Kaul 1982, p. 255.
33 G.S. Bhargava, 'India's Soviet Connection', *The Tribune* (Chandigarh), 2 January 1987.
34 Kaul 1987, p. 17.

35 N.K. Sharma, 'Great and Significant Event', *Soviet Land*, no. 24, December 1986, p. 16.
36 B.M., 'Indo-Soviet Economic Relations: Danger Signals and False Expectations', *EPW*, 25 July 1987, p. 1226.

Chapter 8
1 'Mikhail Gorbachev's Interview with Indonesian Newspaper', *Soviet News*, 29 July 1987, pp. 274–5.
2 Glebov 1987, p. 29.

BIBLIOGRAPHY

Listed below are all works cited in notes. (Newspaper articles and other items identified fully in the text are excluded.) The following abbreviations have been used:

GRVL Glavnaia redaktsiia vostochnoi literatury
M   Moscow
ND   New Delhi

AAS   *Aziia i Afrika segodnia*
AS   *Asian Survey*
EPW   *Economic and Political Weekly*
FEER   *Far Eastern Economic Review*
IAM   *International Affairs* (Moscow)
IDSAJ *Journal* of the Institute for Defence Studies and Analyses (New Delhi)
IQ   *India Quarterly*
IS   *International Studies* (New Delhi)
IT   *India Today*
MEMO   *Mirovaia ekonomika i mezhdunarodnye otnosheniia*
NAA   *Narody Azii i Afriki*
NT   *New Times*
PC   *Problems of Communism*
PH   *Pakistan Horizon*
RS   *Regional Studies* (Islamabad)

Ahmad, Naveed, 1983. 'Indo-Soviet Relations since Mrs Gandhi's Re-election'. *PH*, vol. 36, no. 1, pp. 73–100.

Akhter, Shaheen, 1986. 'Indo-Soviet Economic Relations'. *RS*, vol. 4, no. 3, pp. 81–114.

Alekseev, Aleksandr, 1987. 'The USSR-India: Cooperation for the Benefit of the Peoples'. *IAM*, no. 5, pp. 46–52.

Ali, Mehrunissa, 1983. 'Soviet-Pakistan Ties since the Afghanistan Crisis'. *AS*, vol. 23, no. 9, pp. 1025–42.

Alimov, Iu., 1986. 'Dvizhenie neprisoedineniia v bor'be za delo mira i progressa'. *MEMO*, no. 8, pp. 8–19.

Bach, Quinton V.S., 1987. *Soviet Economic Assistance to the Less Developed Countries*. Oxford: Clarendon.

Banerjee, Jyotirmoy, 1987. 'Moscow's Indian Alliance'. *PC*, vol. 36, no. 1, pp. 1–12.

Bellis, Paul, 1987. 'Third World Review'. *Detente*, nos. 9–10, pp. 42–3.

Belsky, A.G., M.M. Targamadze, and V.V. Chernovskaia, 1987. 'Mezhetnicheskie protivorechiia v Assame i poiski putei ikh preodoleniia'. *NAA*, no. 3, pp. 44–55.

Benevolensky, V.V., 1986. 'Problems of Cooperation and Unity in the Non-Aligned Movement'. In *Soviet Oriental Studies Annual 1986*. M: Nauka, pp. 225–41.

Brezhnev, Leonid I., 1971, 1976, 1981. Report of Central Committee of CPSU to XXIV, XXV and XXVI Congresses of the CPSU, cited according to English editions published by Novosti.

CIA, 1986. *Handbook of Economic Statistics 1986. A Reference Aid*. Washington DC:USGPO. Analogous volumes for earlier years.

Chadda, Maya, 1986. 'India and the United States: Why Detente Won't Happen'. *AS*, vol. 26, no. 10, pp. 1118–36.

Chelyshev, Evgeny, and Aleksei Litman, 1985. *Traditions of Great Friendship*. M: Raduga.

Chicherov, Aleksandr I., 1984. 'South Asia and the Indian Ocean in the 1980s: Some Trends towards Change in International Relations'. *AS*, vol. 24, no. 11, pp. 1117–30.

Clarkson, Stephen, 1973. 'Non-Impact of Soviet Writing on Indian Thinking and Policy'. *EPW*, 14 April, pp. 715–24.

Clarkson, Stephen, 1979. *The Soviet Theory of Development: India and the Third World in Marxist-Leninist Scholarship.* London: Macmillan.

Cohen, Stephen P., 1985. 'South Asia after Afghanistan'. *PC*, vol. 34, no. 1, pp. 18–31.

Communist Party of India (CPI) 1986. *Documents of the 13th Congress of the Communist Party of India. Sohan Singh Josh Nagar, Patna, 12 to 17 March 1986.* ND: CPI.

Communist Party of India (Marxist) (CPI[M]) 1986. *Political Resolution of the Twelfth Congress of the Communist Party of India (Marxist), Calcutta, December 25–30, 1985.* ND: CPI(M).

Damodaran, A.K., 1980. 'Soviet Action in Afghanistan'. *IS*, vol. 19, no. 4, pp. 575–96.

Domenach, Jean-Luc, 1985. 'The Soviet Union and Asia'. *Journal of Communist Studies*, vol. 1, no. 2, pp. 132–51.

Donaldson, Robert H., 1974. *Soviet Policy toward India: Ideology and Strategy.* Cambridge, Mass.: Harvard UP.

———— 1979. *The Soviet-Indian Alignment: Quest for Influence.* Denver, Colo.: University of Denver Graduate School of International Studies.

Dutt, Vidya Prakash, 1984. *India's Foreign Policy.* ND: Vikas.

Frankel, Francine R., 1986. 'Play the India Card'. *Foreign Policy*, no. 62, pp. 148–66.

Fukuyama, Francis, 1987. 'Patterns of Soviet Third World Policy'. *PC*, vol. 36, no. 5, pp. 12–13.

Garev, G., and Iu. Tsaplin, 1981. 'Sovetsko-indiiskaia druzhba – faktor uprocheniia mira'. *MEMO*, no. 7, pp. 17–25.

Gendin, Anatoly A., 1986. 'Kasta i brak v Iuzhnoi Indii'. *NAA*, no. 5, pp. 33–42.

George, Timothy, Robert Litwak, and Shahram Chubin, 1984. *India and the Great Powers.* Aldershot, Hants: Gower for IISS.

Georgiev, Viktor, 1984. 'India: Following a Course of Peace and Independence'. *IAM*, no. 8, pp. 23–31.

———— 1985a. 'India: A Milestone on the Path of Independence'. *IAM*, no. 4, pp. 42–8.

———— 1985b. 'Soviet-Indian Co-operation: Tangible Results and Broad Prospects'. *IAM*, no. 8, pp. 23–9.

141

Georgiev, Viktor, 1986. 'Washington's Strategy in South and Southwest Asia'. *IAM*, no. 12, pp. 57–64.

———— 1987. 'An Event of Historic Significance'. *IAM*, no. 1, pp. 20–7.

Ghosh, Partha S., and Rajaram Panda, 1983. 'Domestic Support for Mrs Gandhi's Afghan Policy: The Soviet Factor in Indian Politics'. *AS*, vol. 23, no. 3, pp. 261–79.

Glebov, Ivan, 1987. 'For New International Relations in Asia and the Pacific'. *IAM*, no. 10, pp. 27–31, 124

———— 1988. 'USSR and India: Cooperation in the Interests of Progress and Peace'. *IAM*, no. 2, pp. 26–32, 49.

Gorbachev, Mikhail S., 1986. *Political Report of the CPSU Central Committee to the 27th Congress of the Communist Party of the Soviet Union. February 25, 1986.* M: Novosti.

Granovsky, A.E., and G.K. Shirikov, 1986. 'Indiia – sovremennyi etap ekonomicheskogo razvitiia'. *MEMO*, no. 6, pp. 65–76.

Griffith, William E., 1982. 'The USSR and Pakistan'. *PC*, vol. 31, no. 1, pp. 38–44.

Gujral, Inder K., 1986. 'Trends in Indo-Soviet Relations'. Pp. 157–65 of *Yearbook on Indian Foreign Policy 1983–84*, ed. Satish Kumar. ND: Sage.

Harrison, Selig S., 1986. 'Cut a Regional Deal'. *Foreign Policy*, no. 62, pp. 126–47.

Hayat, Sikander, 1984. 'Indo-Soviet Relations: New Dimensions'. *RS*, vol. 3, no. 1, pp. 50–71.

Hensel, Howard M., 1985. 'The Soviet Media and Indian Public Opinion'. *The Round Table*, no. 295, pp. 240–55.

Horn, Robert C., 1982. *Soviet-Indian Relations: Issues and Influence.* New York: Praeger.

———— 1983a. 'Afghanistan and the Soviet-Indian Influence Relationship'. *AS*, vol. 23, no. 3, pp. 244–60.

———— 1983b. 'The Soviet Union and Sino-Indian Relations'. *Orbis*, vol. 24, no. 4, pp. 889–906.

———— 1987. 'Soviet Leadership Changes and Sino-Soviet Relations'. *Orbis*, vol. 30, no. 4, pp. 683–99.

Hough, Jerry F., 1986. *The Struggle for the Third World: Soviet Debates and American Options.* Washington DC: Brookings.

Hyman, Anthony, 1986. 'Pakistan in Uncertain Times'. *The World Today*, vol. 42, no. 7, pp. 118–21.

India and the Soviet Union: Co-operation and Development 1975. Ed. Rasheeduddin Khan. Bombay: Allied.

India, Ministry of Planning, Central Statistical Office (CSOP). *Basic Statistics 1985*. ND.

———— *Statistical Abstract. India 1984*. ND, and earlier volumes.

———— *Statistical Pocket Book. India 1985*. ND, and 1984.

Indiia 1980. Ezhegodnik, and analogous volumes for 1981–2, 1983, 1984, and 1985–6. Ed. P.V. Kutsobin. M: GRVL, 1982, 1983, 1985, 1986, 1987.

'Indo-Soviet Economic Relations', 1986. *Spotlight on Regional Affairs* (Islamabad), vol. 5, no. 1, pp. 23–6.

Indo-Soviet Friendship (H.E. Mr Mikhail S. Gorbachev's Visit to India, Nov., 1986) 1986. ND: Ministry of External Affairs.

IISS (International Institute for Strategic Studies), 1987a. *The Military Balance 1987–1988*. London: IISS.

———— 1987b. *Strategic Survey 1986–1987*. London: IISS.

Iurlov, Feliks N., 1987. 'Indiia: 40 let nezavisimosti'. *Kommunist*, no. 12, pp. 116–23.

Iurlova, Evgeniia S., 1986. 'Kasta v politicheskoi zhizni shtata Bikhar (Indiia)'. *NAA*, no. 1, pp. 31–9.

Jetly, Nancy, 1986. 'Sino-Indian Relations: A Quest for Normalization'. *IQ*, vol. 42, no 1, pp. 53–68.

Joshi, Nirmala, 1975. *Foundations of Indo-Soviet Relations: A Study of Non-Official Attitudes and Contacts 1917–1947*. ND: Radiant.

Kadeer, Ahmed A., 1985. 'Soviet-Pakistan Relations: The Ideological Context'. *Journal of European Studies* (Karachi), vol. 1, no. 1, pp. 1–19.

Kamath, P.M., 1984. 'Politics and National Security: American Influence on Indian Thinking'. *IDSAJ*, vol. 16, no. 3, pp. 273–85.

Kapur, Ashok, 1985. 'Indian Foreign Policy: Perspectives and Present Predicaments'. *Round Table*, no. 295, pp. 230–9.

Kapur, Harish, 1987. 'India's Foreign Policy under Indira Gandhi'. *Round Table*, no. 304, pp. 469–80.

Kapur, K.D., 1983. 'Soviet Nuclear Policies in the Third World'. *IQ*, vol. 39, no. 2, pp. 183–92.

Kaul, Triloki Nath, 1982. *Reminiscences, Discreet and Indiscreet.* ND: Lancers.

———— 1987. 'Security in Asia'. *Far Eastern Affairs*, no. 5, pp. 14–19.

Kaushik, Devendra, 1971. *Soviet Relations with India and Pakistan.* ND: Vikas.

———— 1985. 'India, USSR and East Europe: Emerging Trends under Rajiv Gandhi'. *IQ*, vol. 41, no. 1, pp. 6–16.

Kissinger, Henry A., 1979. *The White House Years.* London: Weidenfeld and Nicolson and Michael Joseph.

Kohli, S.N., 1986. 'Indian Ocean: An Area of Tension and Big Power Pressures'. *IQ*, vol. 42, no. 2, pp. 154–65.

Komarov, E., 1987. 'Vdokhnovliaiushchii primer Rossii'. *AAS*, no. 7, pp. 6–9.

Korneev, Viktor L., 1986. *Indiia – 80-e gody.* M: Mysl'.

Kotovsky, Grigory G., 1984. 'Certain Trends in India's Socio-economic and Sociopolitical Development'. *AS*, vol. 24, no. 11, pp. 1131–42.

Kovalenko, Ivan I., 1986. 'A Comprehensive Approach to the Problem of Asian Security'. *Far Eastern Affairs*, no. 2, pp. 14–35.

Kramer, Mark N., 1987. 'Soviet Arms Transfers to the Third World'. *PC*, vol. 33, no. 5, pp. 52–68.

Kreisberg, Paul H., 1986. 'The United States and Asia in 1985: More Problems, Fewer Solutions'. *AS*, vol. 26, no. 1, pp. 1–14.

Kunshchikov, M.N., 1981. *Razvivaiushchiesia strany Azii. Natsional'nye monopolii i politika.* M: Nauka/GRVL.

———— 1986a. 'Natsional'nye monopolii v Indii (pervaia polovina 80-kh godov)'. *NAA*, no. 6, pp. 82–6.

———— 1986b. 'SAARK – Assotsiatsiia regional'nogo sotrudnichestva Iuzhnoi Azii'. *MEMO*, no. 11, pp. 138–40.

Leonidov, M., 1986. "New" Approaches of the USA's Policy towards India'. *IAM*, no. 8, pp. 112–15.

Lifschultz, Lawrence, 1986. 'From the U-2 to the P-3: The US-Pakistan Relationship'. *New Left Review*, no. 159, pp. 71–80.

Litwak, Robert S. and S. Neil MacFarlane, 1987. 'Soviet Activism in the Third World'. *Survival*, vol. 29, no. 1, pp. 21–39.

Losev, Iury, 1987. 'Roads of Friendship'. *IAM*, no. 3, pp. 124–30.

Mansingh, Surjit, 1984. *India's Search for Power: Indira Gandhi's Foreign Policy 1966–1982*. ND: Sage.

Matveev, G.V., 1972. 'Politicheskie makhinatsii Pekina na Indostanskom poluostrove'. *Problemy Dal'nego Vostoka*, no. 4, pp. 39–45.

Mehta, Vinod, 1986. *Development Experience of Soviet Central Asia and the Countries of the Third World*. ND: New Literature.

Mikhin, V., 1986. 'Pakistan – Toeing the Washington Line'. *IAM*, no. 2, pp. 86–90.

Ministerstvo vneshnei torgovli. *Vneshniaia torgovlia SSSR v 1986g. Statisticheskii sbornik*. M: Finansy i statistika, 1987, and earlier volumes.

Mohamedi, Fareed, 1986. 'Indo-Soviet Trade and Payment Relations'. *Wharton Centrally Planned Economies Service*, vol. 6, no. 10.

———— 1987. 'Indo-Soviet Trade and Payment Relations – an Update'. *Wharton Asian Economic Service*, vol. 4, no. 2.

Monthly Public Opinion Survey (MPOS) 1981. 'Popular International Images and Preoccupation with Security'. Blue supplement to *MPOS*, nos. 8–9.

———— 1986. 'A Survey of International Images March-April 1986'. Blue supplement to *MPOS*, nos. 8–9.

Morris-Jones, W.H., 1971. *The Government and Politics of India*. London: Hutchinson.

Mukerjee, Dilip, 1986. 'India and the Soviet Union'. *Washington Quarterly*, vol. 9, no. 2, pp. 109–22.

———— 1987. 'Indo-Soviet Economic Ties', *PC*, vol. 36, no. 1, pp. 13–24.

Naik, J.A., 1970. *Soviet Policy towards India: From Stalin to Brezhnev*. ND: Vikas.

Narain, Iqbal, 1986. 'India in 1985: Triumph of Democracy'. *AS*, vol. 26, no. 2, pp. 253–69.

Narain, Iqbal, and Nilma Dutta, 1987. 'India in 1986: The Continuing Struggle'. *AS*, vol. 27, no. 2, pp. 181–93.

Nossiter, Thomas J., 1982. *Communism in Kerala: A Study in Political Adaptation*. London: Hurst for RIIA.

———— 1985. 'Communism in Rajiv Gandhi's India'. *Third World Quarterly*, vol. 7, no. 4, pp. 924–41.

OECD (Organization for Economic Cooperation and Development), 1986. *1986 Review. Development Co-operation.* Report by Joseph C. Wheeler. Paris: OECD.

Parasher, S.C., 1986. 'Gorbachev Visit: A Historical Perspective'. *IQ*, vol 42, no. 4, pp. 447–58.

Pleshov, Oleg V., 1987. "Islamizatsiia" v Pakistane: motivy i sredstva'. *NAA*, no. 1, pp. 45–54.

Popatia, Mahboob A., 1985. 'The perspectives of Pakistan–Soviet Union Relations'. Pp. 59–146 of *Pakistan Study Centre. Research Series*, vol. 1. Karachi: University of Karachi.

Potter, William C., 1985. 'The Soviet Union and Nuclear Proliferation'. *Slavic Review*, vol. 44, no. 3, pp. 468–88.

Prasad, Bimal, 1980. 'India and the Afghan Crisis'. *IS*, vol. 19, no. 4, pp. 635–41.

Premdev, Jai Prakesh, 1985. *Indo-Soviet Relations.* Meerut and ND: Meenakshi Prakashan.

Rais, Rasul B., 1986. *The Indian Ocean and the Superpowers: Economic, Political and Strategic Perspectives.* London: Croom Helm.

Rajan, M.S., 1985. 'The Seventh Non-Aligned Summit'. Pp. 53–77 of *Yearbook on Indian Foreign Policy 1982–83.* Ed. Satish Kumar. ND: Sage.

Ram, Mohan, 1969. *Indian Communism: Split within a Split.* ND: Vikas.

Remnek, Richard B., 1975. *Soviet Scholars and Soviet Foreign Policy: A Case Study in Soviet Policy towards India.* Durham, NC: Carolina Academic Press.

Reykjavik Summit and Peace in Asia 1986. ND: Allied.

Riabinin, Vladimir, 1986. 'India: Defending National Unity'. *IAM*, no. 12, pp. 119–24.

Rizvi, Gowher, 1987. 'Arms Control and Indo-Pakistani Relations'. In *Arms Control in Asia.* Ed. Gerald Segal. London: Macmillan, pp. 116–43.

Robinson, Thomas W., 1981. 'The Soviet Union and Asia in 1980', *AS*, vol. 21, no. 1, pp. 14–30.

——— 1982. 'The Soviet Union and Asia in 1981'. *AS*, vol. 22, no. 1, pp. 13–32.

Rose, Leo E., 1986. 'United States and Soviet Policy towards South Asia'. *Current History*, vol. 85, no. 509, pp. 97–100, 132–6.

Rubinstein, Alvin Z., 1986. 'Third World Policy Waits for Gorbachev'. *Orbis*, vol. 30, no. 2, pp. 355–64.

Rumiantsev, Y., 1984. 'Model for Fruitful Co-operation'. *IAM*, no. 3, pp. 137–40.

Sager, Peter, 1966. *Moscow's Hand in India: An Analysis of Soviet Propaganda.* Berne: Swiss Eastern Institute.

Sahai-Achuthan, Nisha, 1983. 'Soviet Indologists and the Institute of Oriental Studies: Works on Contemporary India in the Soviet Union'. *Journal of Asian Studies*, vol 42, no. 2, pp. 323–43.

Security without Nuclear Weapons: Indo-Soviet Dialogue 1986. Ed. K. Subrahmanyam and Jasjit Singh. ND: Lancer for IDSA.

Segon, Harish, 1987. 'Rajiv Gandhi's Successful Moscow Visit'. *Indian and Foreign Review*, 31 August, pp. 6–9.

Selbourne, David, 1977. *An Eye to India: The Unmasking of a Tyranny.* Harmondsworth, Middx: Penguin.

Sen Budhraj, Vijay, 1973a. 'Moscow and the Birth of Bangladesh'. *AS*, vol. 12, no. 5, pp. 482–95.

———— 1973b. *Soviet Russia and the Hindustan Subcontinent.* Bombay: Somaiya.

Sen Gupta, Bhabhani, 1972. *Communism in Indian Politics.* New York: Columbia UP.

———— 1976. *Soviet-Asian Relations in the 1970s and Beyond: An Interperceptional Study.* New York: Praeger.

———— 1981. 'Communism and India: A New Context'. *PC*, vol 30, no. 4, pp. 33–45.

Sergiev, Artyom, 1986. 'The Present Stage of the Non-Aligned Movement (The Results of the Eighth Non-Aligned Summit Conference)'. *IAM*, no. 12, pp. 106–13.

Shahi, Agha, 1987. 'Pakistan-Indian Relations and Superpowers' Policy'. *Journal of South Asian and Middle Eastern Studies*, vol. 10, no. 4, pp. 3–16.

Shearman, Peter, 1987. 'Gorbachev and the Third World: An Era of Reform?' *Third World Quarterly*, vol. 9, no. 4, pp. 1083–117.

Shrimali, Shridar, 1986. 'Soviet Example and the Appeal of Socialism in the Third World'. Occasional Paper, Centre for Soviet Studies, University of Bombay.

Shurygin, V., 1987. 'Veka i molodost'. (Indiia. 40 let nezavisimosti)'. *AAS*, no. 8, pp. 17–21.

Singh, Anita Inder, 1988. 'The Soviet Union and India: A Bibliographical Review of Writing in English'. *Journal of Communist Studies*, forthcoming.

Singh, Jasjit, 1985. 'Indian Ocean in Global Strategies – Some Perspectives'. *IDSAJ*, vol. 17, no. 4, pp. 450–79.

Singh, S. Nihal, 1983. 'Can the US and India be Real Friends?' *AS*, vol. 23, no. 9, pp. 1011–24.

———— 1984. 'Why India Goes to Moscow for Arms'. *AS*, vol. 24, no. 7, pp. 707–20.

———— 1986. *The Yogi and the Bear: A Study of Indo-Soviet Relations*. ND: Allied; London: Mansell.

SIPRI Yearbook 1987. World Armaments and Disarmament 1987. Oxford: OUP.

Six Nation Summit on Peace and Disarmament, Ixtapa, Mexico, August 1986. *For a World Free of Nuclear Weapons*. ND: Ministry of External Affairs, 1986.

South Asian Insecurity and the Great Powers 1986. Ed. Barry Buzan and Gowher Rizvi. Basingstoke: Macmillan.

Soviet-American Relations with Pakistan, Iran and Afghanistan. 1987. Ed. Hafeez Malik. Basingstoke: Macmillan.

Soviet Interests in the Third World 1985. Ed. Robert Cassen. London: Sage for RIIA.

SSSR i Indiia 1987. Ed. G.G. Kotovsky, A.N. Kheifets, and P.M. Shastitko. M: GRVL.

Staar, Richard F., 1987. 'Checklist of Communist Parties in 1986'. *PC*, vol. 36, no. 2, pp. 40–56.

Stanislaus, M. Sebastian, 1975. *Soviet Economic Aid to India. An Analysis and Evaluation*. ND: N.V. Publications.

Statistical Outline of India 1986–87. Comp. D.R. Pendse. Bombay: Tata Services.

Tariq Ali, 1985. *The Nehrus and the Gandhis: An Indian Dynasty*. London: Picador.

Tellis, Ashley J., 1986. 'Hawkeyes for Pakistan: Rationale and Logic of the E-2C Request'. *Journal of South Asian and Middle Eastern Studies*, vol. 10, no. 1, pp. 36–66.

Thomas, Raju G.C., 1986. *Indian Security Policy*. Princeton, NJ: Princeton UP.

Thornton, Thomas, 1983. 'The USSR and Asia in 1982: The End of the Brezhnev Era'. *AS*, vol. 23, no. 1, pp. 11–25.

———— 1984. 'The USSR and Asia in 1983: Staying the Brezhnev Course'. *AS*, vol. 24, no. 1, pp. 1–16.

———— 1987. 'Gorbachev's Courtship of India: India and the Soviet Union'. *Round Table*, no. 304, pp. 457–68.

Tomilin, Iury, 1987. 'For a Nuclear-Weapon-Free and Non-Violent World'. *IAM*, no. 3, pp. 3–21, 29.

Travis, Thomas A., 1986. 'United States-Indian Relations: Obstacles and Opportunities'. *IQ*, vol. 42, no. 4, pp. 381–90.

Ulianovsky, Rostislav A., 1983. 'The Indian National Congress: Lessons of Evolution'. *Asia and Africa Today*, no. 1, pp. 16–19.

———— 1986a. 'Aktual'nye problemy natsional'noosvoboditel'-nogo dvizheniia i sotsialisticheskoi orientatsii'. *NAA*, no. 6, pp. 3–13.

———— 1986b. 'Kommunisticheskaia Partiia Indii – partiia patriotov i internatsionalistov'. *NAA*, no. 3, pp. 47–53.

UN 1985. United Nations Conference on Trade and Development. *Handbook of International Trade and Development Statistics. Supplement 1985*. New York: United Nations.

US Arms Control and Disarmament Agency (ACDA) 1987. *World Military Expenditures and Arms Transfers 1986*. Washington DC: ACDA.

US Congress, House, Committee on Foreign Affairs (HFAC) 1985. *The Soviet Union in the Third World 1980–85: An Imperial Burden or Political Asset?* Washington DC: USGPO.

US Congress, Joint Economic Committee 1987, *Gorbachev's Economic Plans*. 2 vols. Washington DC: USGPO.

Valkenier, Elizabeth K., 1986. 'The USSR and the Third World: Economic Dilemmas'. Pp. 731–57 of *Soviet Foreign Policy in a Changing World*. Ed. Robbin F. Laird and Erik P. Hoffmann. Berlin: de Gruyter.

Vanaik, Achin, 1986. 'The Indian Left'. *New Left Review*, no. 159, pp. 49–70.

Vavilov, V., 1986. 'The Solid Foundation for Soviet-Indian Relations'. *IAM*, no. 9, pp. 28–33.

Vivekanandan, B., 1980. 'Afghanistan Invasion Viewed from India'. *Asia Pacific Community*, no. 9, pp. 63–82.

Vizit Prem'era-Ministra Indii M. Desai v Sovetskii Soiuz, 21–26 oktiabria 1977 goda 1977. M: Politizdat.

Wariavwalla, Bharat, 1985. 'Stagnant Indo-Soviet Relations'. *Strategic Analysis*, vol. 9, no. 4, pp. 310–13.

———— 1987. 'The Coming Frost'. *Illustrated Weekly of India*, 25 January, pp. 38–9.

Wirsing, Robert G., 1985. 'The Arms Race in South Asia: Implications for the United States'. *AS*, vol. 25, no. 3, pp. 265–91.

Yearbook on India's Foreign Policy, 1984–85. Ed. Satish Kumar. ND: Sage, 1987.

Zagoria, Donald S., 1985. 'The USSR and Asia in 1984'. *AS*, vol. 25, no. 1, pp. 21–32.

———— 1986. 'The USSR and Asia in 1985: The First Year of Gorbachev'. *AS*, vol. 26, no. 1, pp. 15–29.

Zamostny, Thomas J., 1984. 'Moscow and the Third World: Recent Trends in Soviet Thinking'. *Soviet Studies*, vol. 36, no. 2, pp. 223–35.

Zimbabwe 1987. Ministry of Information. *Eighth NAM Summit Review*. Harare.

14)120